CHRIST'S FAREWELL DISCOURSE

CHRIST'S FAREWELL DISCOURSE

BY

REV. ERNEST LUSSIER, S.S.S.

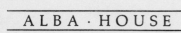

ALBA · HOUSE   NEW · YORK

SOCIETY OF ST. PAUL, 2187 VICTORY BLVD., STATEN ISLAND, NEW YORK 10314

Library of Congress Cataloging in Publication Data

Lussier, Ernest, 1911-
    Christ's Farewell Discourse

    1. Bible. N.T. John XIV-XVII—Criticism,
interpretation, etc. 2. Jesus Christ—Words.
BS2615.2.L87   226'.5'07   79-19798
ISBN: 0-8189-0394-5

Imprimi Potest:
Donald E. Pelotte, S.S.S.
Provincial Superior

Nihil Obstat:
Daniel V. Flynn, J.C.D.
Censor Librorum

Imprimatur:
Joseph T. O'Keefe, Vicar General
Archdiocese of New York
August 7, 1979

The Nihil Obstat and Imprimatur are
a declaration that a book or pamphlet is considered
to be free from doctrinal or moral error. It is not implied
that those who have granted the Nihil Obstat and
Imprimatur agree with the contents,
opinions or statements expressed.

Designed, printed and bound in the United States of
America by the Fathers and Brothers of the
Society of St. Paul, 2187 Victory Boulevard,
Staten Island, New York, 10314, as part of their
communications apostolate.

1 2 3 4 5 6 7 8 9 (Current Printing: first digit).

DEDICATION

AND

FAREWELL

TO ALL

MY FRIENDS AND RELATIVES

EDITOR'S PREFACE

Christ's Farewell Discourse is the last written work of Father Ernest Lussier, S.S.S. While the work is relatively short the author in his own opinion, felt the work is the best that he has put forth, and has dedicated it as a farewell to all his friends and relatives. Like Christ's discourse this work too is a parting legacy. Already when this book was undertaken, that is to prepare the manuscript, Father began even the more momentous task of preparing to die. On Palm Sunday, 1978 he learned that he was terminally ill. In October he submitted the manuscript to his Provincial Superior, requesting permission for its publication. He indicated to his Superior that his long stint of writing was now concluded and that he would spend the remaining time in preparation to meet the Lord.

On March 9, 1979 he was called from this life after a yearlong bout with cancer, which had inexorably taken its toll. I was one of the concelebrants of his funeral Mass at St. Jean the Baptiste in Manhattan. This Church is well known as a center for daily Solemn Exposition and Adoration of the Blessed Sacrament. The Church is staffed by the Congregation of the Blessed Sacrament, of which Father Lussier was a member. His own life was particularly characterized by his love for the Eucharist, the Bible and the priesthood. This found expression in many years of teaching, followed by a very prolific period of writing.

From 1939 to 1972 he taught Scripture in major seminaries, in Cleveland, Ohio and Mundelein, Illinois. From

1974 until 1978 he was a staff-contributor to *Emmanuel* magazine, and had eight books accepted for publication, including this—his last. Alba House published his trilogy which dealt with the Eucharist: *Getting to Know the Eucharist, Living the Eucharistic Mystery,* and *The Eucharist: the Bread of Life; God is Love,* and two major works on the subject of adoration: *Adore the Lord* and *Jesus Christ is Lord.* Father's works have a value that is lasting and classical, since all of these have been written with a sound biblical expertise and an exhaustive effort to extricate the complete Biblical message.

In the Father's house there are many dwelling places (Jn 14:2). We trust that the author has earned a most unique place through his special contribution to make known the Good News. The message of this book was pondered in faith and suffering, hopeful that the reader will renew his or her own faith in God's plan for our salvation.

Staten Island, N.Y.   Anthony L. Chenevey, S.S.P.
May 15, 1979   Editor

CONTENTS

CHRIST'S LAST DISCOURSE

Jesus' farewell discourse (Jn Ch 13-17) is an interpretation of Jesus' completed work on earth and of his relation to both believers and the world after his resurrection. It is possible that the discourse is based on several homilies given by John at the Eucharist, which were pieced together for inclusion in his gospel. Jn 13:31-38 is the prelude to Christ's Last Discourse.

John's gospel is frequently analyzed into the Book of Signs (1:19-12:50), and the Book of Glory (13:1-20:31), with a prologue and an epilogue. For John a sign is an act of power by Jesus which points to a truth inaccessible to sight and touch, but apprehensible by faith. Paradoxically, glory, an Old Testament term signifying God's presence, is for the evangelist publicly manifest in the earthly career of Jesus, who to the eyes of faith reveals himself as Son of God in certain significant events, especially through his death and resurrection.

In the Book of Signs, John narrates first the story of Jesus' sign and follows this with a discourse interpreting the sign, for example in Ch 6. In the Book of Glory the pattern is reversed. Christ's Last Discourse explains the significance of his deeds, namely, his return to the Father, his passion, death, and resurrection; but it precedes what it explains. It would have been awkward to do otherwise. And in any case, the disciples would be affected by Jesus' passion and death, and had to be prepared for this by Jesus' explanation and consolation.

Jesus' farewell discourse and prayer (Ch 14-17) is an interpretation of Jesus' completed work on earth and of his relation to both believers and the world after his resurrection and ascension. It is a meditation, which, like a love letter is difficult to outline. The overall run of the thought, however, is clear enough. First the coming departure of Jesus and the future of the disciples (13:31-14:31); then the life of the disciples and their encounter with the world, after Jesus shall have departed (Ch 15-16); finally, the concluding prayer of Jesus (Ch 17). There is an appropriate and natural progression in the discourse: first, talk with individual disciples, then Jesus' soliloquy, then the great prayer.

In this most sublime of farewells, Jesus, on the eve of his visible departure from this world, consoles and strengthens his first disciples, and through them, us. There are no logical divisions, no systematic developments, but always the same spiral, circling movements of the eagle, the same recurring thoughts progressively strengthened and deepened: the Father mentioned some forty times, going to the Father, coming, seeing, knowing, believing, loving, the Spirit, life, truth, abiding, peace, joy, fruitfulness, prayer, persecutions from the world, unity, glory. Jesus is as one still in the world, yet not of it. He speaks of the heights of spirituality: the life and action together of the divine persons, the intimate relations between them and believers, between himself and the Paraclete and again between them and the Christians of the future. The other discourses of Jesus in John are to hostile audiences; this alone is to intimate friends.

Although we cannot think of these words as being remembered verbatim, no mind other than our Lord's could have conceived them. In their present setting between the Last Supper and the cross, they convey an imperishable impression of the range and depth of our Lord's teaching. These are chapters to be read and re-read, and nothing in the

New Testament will bring us closer to the mind of Christ. Here are not only great themes (especially peace, love, and unity), but great sayings: "I am the way, and the truth, and the life" (Jn 14:6); "he who has seen me, has seen the Father" (14:9); "Greater love than this no man has, that a man lay down his life for his friends" (15:13); "I have overcome the world" (16:53); "I pray that they all may be one" (17:21). Here too is our Lord's teaching on the Spirit, who will guide the Church in all truth (16:13), and his matchless prayer of self-consecration as he turns to face his cross (17:1-16).

Christ's farewell discourse contains some of the most typical ideas to be found in the gospel, namely: Jesus' anticipation of the glory of his finished work, the law of love which is to be the rule of his Church, and the trials which will drive his disciples to complete reliance on him. The language and the thought of this section are alike conspicuous. The marvel of it is that it meets our needs and answers our questions as fully as it met the needs and answered the questions of the twelve in the Cenacle and of the Christians of the first century. Some themes are repeated: Christ's impending death, his bodily departure and continued presence, the consequences of these events for the life and mission of the disciples, both in their inner corporate community and in their outward witness to the world. The evangelist always anticipates themes for further comment, and in fact, this intertwining of present and future gives the discourse a dramatic tension.

Christ's Last Discourse belongs to the literary genre of the farewell speech. This had already made its appearance in the earlier books of the Old Testament, for instance, the farewell and blessings of Jacob to his children (Gn 47:29-49:33); Joshua's farewell to Israel (Jos 22-24); David's farewell in 1 Ch 27-29. Perhaps the most important example from the pre-exilic period would be Deuteronomy where the whole book is made up of Moses' farewell speeches to Israel. This literary genre became even more popular in the late biblical and the intertestamental periods. In the New Testament the speech of Paul to the elders of Ephesus (Ac

20:17-38) is a type of farewell speech. This genre is also attested in the epistolary literature; for instance the Pastoral Epistles are a form of Pauline farewell (especially 2 Tm 3:1-4:8), and 2 P is a form of Petrine farewell. Finally, our Lord's Farewell Discourse corresponds in many ways to the apocalyptic discourse before his passion (Mk 13). It deals, albeit in a very different style and manner, with the imminent departure of Jesus and the consequent fate of his disciples, and with his return to them in succor and deliverance.

Although Jesus speaks at the Last Supper, he is really speaking from heaven; his words are directed to Christians at all times. The Last Discourse is Jesus' last testament; it is meant to be read after he has left the earth. It has been transformed in the light of the resurrection and through the coming of the Holy Spirit, into a living discourse delivered not by a dead man, but by one who has life, to all readers of the gospel. In it Jesus speaks as one already glorified, for the chain of events connected with his glorification has now begun.

The Farewell Discourse contains meditations upon sayings of Jesus composed at different times and strung together without any organic unity. Thus in Ch 14-16 we have sayings about the Paraclete side by side with other sayings. The climax of these meditations is reached in the great prayer of Ch 17, where the mystical union of the Church with its Lord, and the unity of its members severally with one another are rooted in the fellowship within the Godhead. John has not planned the whole complex as a unity; the contents are loosely strung together with very little progression of thought, however the chapters are arranged.

Accepting the existing order, it can be supposed that the discourse is based on several homilies, which John has pieced together for inclusion in the gospel. The sources would be in fact John's own homilies. This theory that the Supper Discourse is based on homilies at the Eucharist, disposes of the problem of historicity. We need not suppose that they were actually spoken by Jesus in the course of the Last Supper. Like the other discourses of the fourth Gospel, they would be John's own composition on the basis of his Eucharistic homilies which are in substance the traditional words and teachings of Jesus not necessarily tied to this occasion. John introduced in this Last Discourse of Jesus words that express with great clarity the intentions and the will of the Master concerning the condition of the believing community during the period which begins with his elevation to glory.

The episode of the footwashing and the sayings that are joined to it, form the prelude to the long conversations between Jesus and his disciples. In their actual form Ch 13-17 group together teaching probably given by Jeus on other occasions. Ch 16 is a rather complex presentation and probably gives a new version of the words of Jesus found in Ch 14. Grouping them in this fashion, John intends to show the deep meaning of all the life of Jesus at the time when he is about to pass from his earthly to his heavenly existence.

Jn 13:31-38 is the prelude to the Last Discourse (Ch 14-17). It introduces the theme of Jesus' departure (13:31-33), focuses on Christ's commandment of love (34-35), and foretells Peter's denial (36-38). Jesus' glorification, which is the goal of the hour, is an appropriate opening theme for the great discourse explaining the hour. This glorification involves his return to his Father and, therefore, his departure from his disciples (33). The command to love (34-35) is Jesus' way of ensuring the continuance of his spirit among his disciples.

"Now when Judas had gone, Jesus said, Now is the Son of Man glorified, and in him God is glorified; and if God is glorified in him, God will also glorify him in himself, and glorify him at once. Little children, yet a little while I am with you. You will seek me; and as I said to the Jews, so now I say to you: where I am going you cannot come" (13:31-33). Jesus begins to prepare his disciples for losing him. He puts aside his own sorrow to lighten theirs. He uses a tender form of address (little children) found only in this gospel. As he thinks of them his manner changes from the didactic to the paternal. They will miss him and cannot follow him now, but their case

will not be that of the Jews. They will have a common love-tie
in him. Christ's departure and his glorification are intimately
related. For the Jews the separation will be final (8:21); for the
disciples only for a while (14:2-3). "You cannot come" except
by dying.

The glorification of the Son is also that of the Father; the
one is effected in the other. This glorification will occur
immediately; though the perspective of Jesus' glorification in
the parousia is also found in John, his emphasis is on realized
eschatology. The passion has already begun since Judas has
just gone out to do Satan's work; Jesus speaks of his victory
as already won. The eschatological now appears as an
exchange; Jesus glorifies the Father by his perfect obedience
in humble service unto death; the Father answers by
associating him to himself, by making him share in his eternal
glory by the resurrection and exaltation to his right. The Son of
Man already glorified by miracles (2:11, 14:4) has as supreme
glory to be lifted up on the throne of the cross and so ascend to
his Father. He has always sought the Father's glory, but will
give him perfect glory by the obedient, loving sacrifice of his
life. It is in Jesus crucified that God reveals his glory: in his
turn Jesus will gain glory in God, as he is exalted as Son of
Man to the glory of the Father. As God is glorified in the
Messianic work of the Son, so the Son shall be glorifed in the
eternal blessedness of the Father.

"A new commandment I give you, that you love one
another; even as I have loved you, that you also love one
another. By this all men will know that you are my disciples, if
you love one another" (34-35). Judas had displayed the evil
born of self-centeredness. Jesus was about to show them his
undiluted love for the Father in obedience to his will. He is to
leave them physically, and the only bond which will keep
them together is love, fostered within them by the Spirit. The
death that Judas has gone to arrange will glorify, that is,
reveal the essence of both the Father and the Son as holy love.
The disciples are now the organ of this love.

The reference to Christ's departure makes this commandment of Christian love Christ's testament. Though enunciated in the Mosaic Law, Christ's command is new in its extension to all men without distinction (Lk 10:29-37) and in the ideal it strives to emulate (15:13). It is new because Jesus sets the standard so high by telling his followers to love one another as he himself loved them, and because love is to be the distinguishing mark of the new era which the death of Jesus inaugurates and proclaims to the world. The command is described as new not because nothing like it has ever been uttered, but because it reflects the relations within the Godhead, the mutual love existing between the Father and the Son (15:12-15), and still more because it belongs to the new age which the work of Jesus introduced. There is to be a new love-circle depending on a new love center, Christ.

Christ's love is not only the model and measure of Christian love but also its motive and cause, its source and spirit. Jesus' death for his friends (15:13) makes the observance of the new commandment of love possible. Christ more than fulfilled the Mosaic precept; he not only loved his neighbor as himself, but he loved him more than himself, for he laid down his life for men. New refers to the new situation which is created by the sacrifice of Christ, in which the conditions of the age to come are already anticipated. Love is the fulfilling of the law. The old commandment to love one another (Lv 19:18), which our Lord regarded as an essential feature of the law, is now reenacted in a higher sense, and grounded on a new motive, the love of Christ for all mankind, as shown in his atoning death. The Eucharist, the feast which commemorates this death, is to be the great bond of love and union among Christians. To love one another is the moral consequence of table fellowship.

The mutual love of the disciples is the rule for the new era, when the Father and the Son are glorified in each other, and so constitutes the earthly counterpart to their relationship. Christian love is not to be limited to Christians, but among Christians it has the special function of mirroring the love of the divine Persons for one another and for the

Church. Love finds its full expression in a community where there is exchange, gift of self, and receptivity, acceptance of others.

This love between Christians is the mark by which Jesus' disciples are to be recognized. "See how these Christians love one another" (Tertullian). Charity, "the love and image of Christ the Savior in us" (Clement of Alexandria), "opens hearts and wins them to the truth more than miracles" (Chrysostom). It comes from God who is love, and his Spirit of love, and is manifested in doing good with self-sacrifce. This is the true note of the Church, not miracles, formularies, or numbers, but love. Jesus could never have set a higher pattern before his people than this. A living brotherly love is par excellence the sign of the presence of the love of God in our life, hence the importance of fraternal love as a sign of the Church waiting for Christ.

13:36 is a veiled prophecy of Peter's martyrdom. He is not yet ready to follow Jesus to death; afterward, according to tradition, he was martyred. His statement, "I will lay down my life for you," is an expression of loyalty but also, in the actual circumstances, imaginative heroism. Jesus allowed Peter's fall so that when he became head of the Church he might know how to be humble and have pity on sinners. So much for fine resolutions without a prayer for help.

JESUS, THE WAY

Jn Ch 14 begins with a note of reassurance that the disciples will not be separated from Jesus. He goes ahead to prepare a place for them in his Father's house, and he will return to take them with him. He is the way to the Father (Jn 14:1-7).

The narrative of the Last Supper (Jn Ch 13) is concerned with the meaning of discipleship. The final section (13:31-38) introduces briefly themes of crucial importance for the well-being of the Christian community. These cry out for further expansion and explanation. We know that the departure of Jesus (13:33) means his return to the Father, but we need to know what that means for those whom he must leave behind. Jesus has given the commandment to love one another (13:34), but has not gone into this in detail. Nor has he shown how the disciples' behavior is to be a witness to the world (13:35). Peter has been told that he will follow the Master afterward, even perhaps by the way of martyrdom (13:36), but as the passion of Jesus is a unique event, we need to know what this means in the practical life of the Church. It is obvious that the essential point which must be established is the precise relationship of the disciples to Jesus in his state of glory. It must also be shown how they are to carry on the work of his mission, which has been accomplished in one sense, but still remains to be begun as far as the Gentiles are concerned. These are all matters of contemporary concern.

A quick glance through the contents of Jesus' Last Discourse shows that they correspond with 13:31-38 in the reverse order. Ch 14 answers Peter's question, "Where are you going?" Jesus goes to the Father (14:1-11). His departure entails a new relationship between him and his disciples. His earthly mission will be accomplished through them (14:12-14) with the aid of "another Paraclete" (14:15-17). They will not be separated from him, but will share in his own relationship with the Father, expressed in terms of indwelling (14:18-24). These facts about the future are made known in advance, so as to sustain the disciples at the time of the shattering experience of the death of Jesus, which is imminent at the time of speaking (14:25-31).

With Ch 15 we come to the exposition of the commandment to the disciples to love one another (13:34-35). This consists of the allegory of the vine (15:1-17). Moreover just as the love of the brethren is to be a witness to the world (13:35), so the work of the disciples under the Paraclete's guidance will make an impact on the world, including the real possibility of martyrdom (15:18-16:15). At 16:16 we come to an exposition of the intentionally obscure "little while" of 13:33. This again, like the conclusion of Ch 14, leads to an assurance that all shall be well, an assurance that can carry the disciples through the time of testing. Finally, Ch 17, the prayer of Jesus, takes up the thought of glorifying the Son of Man (13:31-32).

The introduction (13:31-38) announced the theme of Jesus' departure; what follows in the Last Discourse is concerned with answering the problems raised by this departure; not the problems of what will happen to Jesus (only his glorification is mentioned) but the problems of what will happen to the disciples he leaves behind. Ch 14 tackles these problems more directly than do the other parts of Ch 15 and Ch 16. It begins with the note of reassurance that the disciples will not be separated from Jesus. He will return to take them with him (3); their requests will be answered by his

Father and by him (12-13); the Paraclete will come to them as
a form of Jesus' continued presence (16-17, 26); Jesus
himself will come back to them (18); and so will his Father
come to them (23). Finally, the chapter returns to the theme of
reassurance (27-29).

Our Lord offers words of consolation. The disciples have
been told that Jesus will leave them and will be betrayed by
one of themselves. We may suppose a sad silence. Then
Jesus goes straight to the leitmotif of all his encouragement,
confident faith which they must have in God and in himself.
Next he raises their troubled minds to his Father's house,
whither he goes to prepare them places, and whence he will
come to bring them with him (1-4); the way is himself (5-11);
he will enable them to do greater things than he has done (12-
14), will send them the Paraclete (15-17) to guide them (25-
26), will himself be living and present to all who love him (18-
24) and will give them his peace and joy (27-29).

Ch 14 is not easily susceptible of formal division. It raises
up the main themes of the Last Discourse: the departure and
return of Jesus; the heavenly abodes; Christ as the way to the
Father, as the revelation of the Father; the mutual indwelling
of the Son, and of the believers in him, with the Father; the
efficacy of prayer through Christ; the promise and mission of
the Paraclete; the obedience of the believer to Christ in love.
Briefly, it focuses on the believer's relation to the glorified
Christ; it is not separation but deepened fellowship. "Let not
your hearts be troubled" (14:1). This reassurance is picked up
again at the end of the chapter (27). It sets the tone of the
whole Last Discourse.

The apostles are perturbed by the predictions of betrayal,
of Christ's departure, and of Peter's denial. Jesus wants to
strengthen their faith. "You believe in God, believe also in
me" (14:1). This purpose pervades Ch 14. Jesus comforts his
disciples by showing them that his departure will establish a
more intimate communion with him and the Father, and with
the assurance of the Spirit's protection. Believe is the sum of
all the discourse, and it is urged until they did believe (16:30);

then our Lord prays and departs. The secret of the untroubled heart is a firmer faith. Faith is the armor and consolation of the soul and of life.

Previously we have heard that Jesus was troubled in facing death (11:33, 13:21), seemingly because death belongs to the realm of Satan. Putting Jesus to death will be the final act of hostility between the world and the disciples who follow Jesus. Thus the troubling of the disciples' hearts is part of the dualistic struggle between Jesus and the prince of this world. In this light Jesus' demand that they have faith in him is more than a request for a vote of confidence; the disciples' faith conquers the world by uniting them to Jesus who has conquered the world (16:33). The distress of the disciples is occasioned especially by the premonition of Jesus' death, but this is scarcely distinguished from their bewilderment at his speaking of it in terms of withdrawal, and this in its turn reflects the problem of the Church serving an apparently absent Master.

The Christian message to perplexed, disquieted, and doubting men is: believe in the kind of God made known to us by Jesus, the kind of God he himself knew and obeyed. It is the inseparability of these two beliefs that the Church has, despite every false emphasis, sought to maintain in her dogmatic Trinitarian and Christological statements. Faith, which is confidence based on God revealing himself and assuring us of his help, will necessarily surmount anxiety. Henceforth, it will also be faith in Jesus, the Incarnate Son, in whom we receive the supreme, the ultimate revelation. A genuine belief in God leads to belief in his Son. Belief in God has new meaning in Jesus. The theme that faith in God has its counterpart faith in Jesus reappears in terms of knowing and seeing (7, 9). One and the same faith is involved.

The antidote to sorrow is faith. Our death is a home-coming. The metaphors of going and coming are gradually spiritualized into the expression of abiding presence: "that where I am you also may be" (14:3). In his Father's house there is room for all, and Jesus is going ahead to prepare for us. We may recall how Jesus, the day before (Mk 14:12-16), had sent two of his disciples ahead to secure a large upper room for the Last Supper. They did not know the way but had to follow the owner. Arriving they found everything prepared, as Jesus had said. It looks as if here Jesus has made the disciples' journey of the previous day into a parable of eternity, in which the upper room foreshadows the home of God with rooms for all. The rooms represent abiding places, symbolic of ample spiritual provision which God makes for his children. The point here is not degrees in heaven but plenty of room, and the fact is stressed by its repetition in a negative form: "If it were not so I should have told you, for I am going to prepare a place for you" (14:2).

By his passion, glorification, and the sending of the Spirit, the Son of the house (8:35-36) prepares eternal life for us. By his passage to glory, Jesus assures for all believers the possibility of enjoying forever communion with God. For him to go, through death and resurrection to his Father's house was to prepare a place of permanent fellowship with him. Jesus has been rejected by the stewards of God's house on earth, but has full access to the eternal counterpart in heaven.

The house being the place where one has a permanent residence, the expression, house of God, was applied to the temple which was the place of God's special presence among his people; the image was then used to express the transcendence of the divine existence; thus one says symbolically that God's house is fixed in heaven. How simple and childlike is this picture. The ideas of Father, house, home, rest have all entered into the world's language. Heaven is where God dwells and manifests himself. There we shall have a Father's love and care; every want will be supplied; sorrow and pain will be unknown.

"And when I go and prepare a place for you, I will come again and will take you to myself, that where I am you also may be" (14:3). This promise keeps the Church's hope alive. The departure of Jesus implies his return. The return of Jesus to associate his disciples in his glorious condition will take place at the end of time, but it is anticipated even now in the time of the Church. This coming again is not always the same throughout this discourse; it is either the resurrection, or the gift of the Paraclete, or the death of individuals, or the presence of Christ in his Church, or the second advent at the last day. Jesus will return to his friends after the crucifixion (19). Jesus and his Father will come to abide with those who love Jesus and keep his word (21, 23); not a public manifestation but a manifestation in faith. This abiding presence of Christ is effected by the Paraclete (16-17, 26). Though Jesus thus comes in the present, it remains true that he will come, though no attempt is made to say when this future coming will take place (3). The whole discourse considers jointly these moments of the coming of the risen Christ, hence the surprising mixture of presents and futures.

For the disciples the saying probably meant primarily, I will return on earth with the Messianic kingdom; later it would be interpreted of the spiritual union between himself in heaven and them on earth, they already risen with him, and he already dwelling in them; and beyond both of these the union between him and them, when both had passed through death and they were once more with him. All this fullness of meaning must have been implicit in the Lord's vision. The metaphor is continued: Jesus will go first and prepare the rooms, and then come back to welcome the guests. It is natural to think of this as the Parousia, or Second Coming. But if Jesus' departure is his death, then the return is his resurrection, and the reception of the guests is the mutual indwelling which will obtain in the post-resurrection situation of the Church (23). The final thought here is certainly eschatological: the second advent of Christ. But that by no means exhausts what Jesus is saying. Jesus will come again especially in the Spirit (18, 21, 23). There is no vacuum between the days of his flesh and the final arrival in the Father's house.

"And you know the way where I am going" (14:4). Jesus had repeatedly told them that he is going to the Father, and in what way, namely through his sacrificial death (12:23-32), which is in turn the model that all must take who would follow him. The stress on the way is important. All John's religious contemporaries would have agreed with him that it was essential that the soul should find its way out of its evil environment into heaven and to God. Many shared Thomas' bewilderment. "Thomas said to him, Lord we do not know where you are going; how can we know the way? Jesus said to him, I am the way, and the truth, and the life. No one can come to the Father, but by me. If you had known me, you would have known my Father also; henceforth you know him and have seen him" (14:5-7). Jesus is the way to the Father; access to God is solely through him. Jesus answers Thomas' question by specifying the destination as the Father, and the means of access as Jesus himself. Thus the center of interest has been shifted from Jesus' personal going, that is, the passion, to the going of the disciples which is the Christian way of life.

The image of the way, hard and difficult which Israel must travel at God's call and relying on faith in him, in view of reaching the promised land, belongs to the symbolics of the Exodus. The metaphor was later applied to the Law, which reveals the orientations which the Lord proposes to his people in view of eternal rewards. In the New Testament the image persists but is transformed. Jesus inaugurates a new way of walking to God and according to God, so that early Christianity was called the Way. In John the expression takes on a deeper meaning: Jesus is not only the way because of his teaching which leads to life; he is the way that leads to the Father because he himself is the truth and the life.

Jesus is the way: in him we have access to the Father; he makes the Father known to the world; he comes from the Father and goes to the Father and is one with him. He is the truth, the total reality of the gift of the Father and of his saving plan. In him is realized what was announced by the law. He proclaims the words he has received from the Father who sent him. He helps us to know the Father whom he knows, and invites us to give him our faith. He is the true light. After his glorification the Spirit of truth will guide believers to the total truth. The believer who is in the truth is sanctified by it, abides in it, does it. He adores the Father in Spirit and in truth.

Jesus is also the life. God is the absolute master of life and has transmitted its mastery to his Son. The Son who is himself life, has life in himself and gives it to those who believe in him. This life is symbolized by water and nourished by the bread of life (faith and the Eucharist). It is often qualified as eternal life, to denote a strictly divine quality by which this life is beyond what is corporal, beyond time and measurable duration. It is promised to believers but is already given to them and will be perfected in the resurrection.

There is here gathered in one pregnant utterance the whole mind and mission of Jesus. A way unites two places; its function is to heal divisions, to bridge gulfs of separation, to lead men home. Jesus is the way uniting two worlds, bridging the gulf of separation between time and eternity, between God and man. Truth is correspondence with reality. God is reality, and Jesus is truth because he knows God. In him there is perfect correspondence with God. It is not just that Jesus speaks the truth: he is the truth. All the real questions of men are answered, not only by what Jesus says in speech, but especially by what he is in his essential being. He did not answer all our speculative questions. But his life is the answer to all the final questions. He is the truth about God and about human life itself; he is the truth by which man lives and dies. It is the Incaranate Word who gives meaning to life and to the universe. It is within the context of incarnational belief that the questions involved in life receive the only really satisfactory and satisfying answer. So, also, Jesus is the life, life in its essence. He is the way to life, and the truth about life, because he is life itself.

The way is the primary predicate; the truth and the life are explanations of the way. Jesus is the way because he is the truth or revelation of the Father, so that when men know him they know the Father (7) and when men see him they see the Father (8). He is the way because he is the life, since he lives in the Father and the Father lives in him (10-11), he is the channel through which the Father's life comes to men. The Imitation of Christ beautifully paraphrases the reply of Jesus: "Without the way, there is no going; without the truth, there is no knowing; without the life, there is no living. I am the way you ought to follow; the truth you ought to trust; the life you ought to hope for. I am the only way, the infallible truth, the endless life."

PRAYER IN JESUS' NAME

No one can see the Father except as revealed in his Son (Jn 14:9). The mission of the disciples is grounded on the power of their belief in Jesus (14:12-14). Christian prayer is addressed to God in Jesus' name (14:13). It is a form of prayer which arises from Jesus' glorification and the gift of the Spirit (14:15-17).

Christ's words of consolation to his disciples are based on his relation to the Father (Jn 14:8-11). Knowledge of God is solely through the person, words, and works of Jesus. Philip expresses man's deepest aspiration, one which nothing less than God can satisfy. "Lord, show us the Father, and we shall be satisfied" (14:8). Philip, who like Thomas is sense-bound, protests that seeing is believing. This is an expression of the unsatisfied longing of the Old Testament (Ex 33:18-19), which, however, association with Christ should have removed long before. Philip asks for some kind of extraordinary manifestation, but he must learn that the only vision of God vouchsafed in this world is through Jesus Christ.

The difficulty of Philip is expressed in words which voice the deepest need of humanity. He had seen without seeing. Physical sight is not spiritual sight. He asks for a theophany. If he can only have a physically visible manifestation of the Father, he thinks his mind will be satisfied. Blinding and deluding thought. A God who could be seen in this way would be no God; as a God who could be defined would no longer be God. In every age men delude themselves with the notion that if they could have an indisputable sign of God to their physical senses, or an irrefragable proof of God to their intellects, they would be satisfied. They do not know that religion is life, and its own sign and own proof. There is a sign and a proof that springs out of religion itself, namely faith (Heb 11:1).

"He who has seen me has seen the Father" (14:9). No man can see God except as revealed. He is revealed in his Son. Christ's wondrous life is the all-sufficing revelation. The Son is the visible face of the Father. To see God is blessedness; to see Christ is to see God; to see God in Christ is heaven. Look for no sign in the heavens or on the earth. Say with the Greek of an earlier chapter, "We would see Jesus." Whoever in faith knows and sees Jesus, whoever experiences the life of grace and is witness to Christ living and acting in his Church, has already achieved the heavenly goal, which is to know and to see God. All the life of Jesus, his words and actions were the perfect manifestation of the Father, because he is united to him in indescribable communion. It is evidently not said, however, that henceforth God is replaced by the man Jesus. In seeing Jesus one sees God. The Johannine stress on the oneness of Jesus and the Father is primarily related to the Son's mission to men, and has only secondary metaphysical implications about life within the Godhead. Because Jesus is an agent who is God's own Son, John deepens the legal relationship of agent and sender (the one who is sent is completely representative of the one who sends him) to a relationship of likeness of nature.

"Do you not believe that I am in the Father and the Father in me?" (14:10). When Philip asks for some special manifestation of the Father, he is falling short of that faith by which alone the Father is seen to be in the Son and the Son in the Father. This unity of the Father and the Son is the very being of Jesus, but only faith can discern the glory of God in the face of Christ (2 Cor 4:6). Both his words and his works, revelatory and full of power, are his Father's, for his Father is in him.

To claim that God may be seen in Jesus is substantiated by the relationship between them. This is a relationship of mutual indwelling. Jesus on his side never speaks on his own authority, as he says repeatedly, but only and wholly in obedience to the Father. The Father on his side does his works, is active in the world, in and through Jesus. So by the submission of himself to the Father, and by the Father's initiative in working through him, Jesus can claim to be the revelation of the Father. The exact nature of the mutual indwellling is not defined. It is not merely a mystical union, comparable to the experience of the mystics, implying absorption in the divine. It is, first of all, a moral union, the supreme example of the relationship which the disciples themselves may expect to have with God. But it is also a metaphysical union in which Jesus is differentiated from all other men, by the fact that he is the self-expression of God.

The mission of the disciples and the power of belief in Jesus are described in (14:12-14). "He who believes in me will also do the works that I do; and greater works than these will he do, because I go to the Father" (14:12). Christ brought revelation and salvation; his miracles were signs of these things. The works of the disciples will continue this ministry. The Spirit, from whom mighty words will proceed, is to be sent by Jesus seated in glory at the Father's right hand. The greater deeds of Christian activity remain the works of Christ himself, for he will give the power by which they are done. Faith is the key to all Jesus is saying. And just as faith in the historical Jesus as God's Son rested upon his words and his works, which testified to him because they were really God's words and works, in the same way faith in the Christ of the Church rests on the works of the Christian faithful which are really Christ's.

These greater works are not more astounding miracles but wider opportunities, even more plainly revealing the purpose of God, that is, the gathering of many believers into the Church. Our Lord is always kindling in his followers the expectation of greater results. It was so during his lifetime (1:51, 5:20); it will be so after he has gone. These greater works are also works of a more exalted nature because redemption is achieved. They will be done by the believers through prayer (13, 15) obedience (15) and the Holy Spirit (16-17).

"Whatever you ask in my name, I will do it, that the Father may be glorified in the Son" (14:13). The name designated the person of Christ in his glorious condition, and connotes the spiritual power which transforms men's lives. The disciples will perform the great works announced if they ground themselves on him and ask him to accomplish them. The action of Jesus in answer to prayer manifests the glory, or spiritual power, which the Father has given to the Son, and consequently works also for the Father's glory. Not only is Christian prayer to be offered in the name of, that is, invoking the mediation of the Son, but even answers to prayer are given through the Son, that the same honor may be accorded to the Son as to the Father.

In prayer the Jews frequently recalled the patriarchs in the hope that God would be touched by the remembrance of those holy men, and prayer in Jesus' name may have originated in similar manner. The Eucharist, which was celebrated in remembrance of Jesus, may have contributed to the custom of praying in the name of Jesus, especially since early Christian prayers would frequently be voiced on the occasion of the Eucharist. But Johannine theology has introduced into prayer in Jesus' name an emphasis that goes beyond the use of a formula. A Christian prays in the name of Jesus in the sense that he is in union with Jesus. Because the Christian is in union with Jesus, and Jesus is in union with the Father, there can be no doubt that the Christian's request will be granted. This context of union with Jesus also suggests that the requests of the Christian are now no longer thought of as requests concerning petty things of life; they are requests of such a nature that when they are granted the Father is glorified in the Son (13). They are requests pertinent

to the Christian life and to the continuation of the work by
which Jesus glorified the Father during his ministry (17:4).

Jesus' works are always the result of prayer, which
expresses the unity of his will with the Father's. In the same
way the disciples' continuation of his mission depends on
prayer and naturally is done in his name. To pray in the name
of Jesus implies a communion of persons; harmony of will
with God and obedience to his commandments are necessary
conditions for efficacious prayer. By "in my name" is not of
course meant the mere using the formula "Through Jesus
Christ." It means praying and working as Christ's representative, in the same spirit in which Christ prayed and worked,
acting in his spirit and carrying on his work, in accordance
with his character and will. To pray in the name of Jesus is to
pray in full faith as to who he is, his revelation about himself
and his relations to us.

"In my name" firmly grounds the promise in the
condition of faith which leaves the initiative with Christ. The
secret of our Christian power is our constant communion with
the Father through his Son. The secret of having, in that
spiritual relation, is asking, and Christ challenges his
disciples to ask what they will in his name. It is as if his credit
in God's bank were made our checking account; only we must
not draw a check which we cannot ask him to countersign.
This communion is to be realized through the obedience
which is the test of love. His love commands and delights to be
asked; ours should ask and delight to be commanded.

The name signifies the reality suggested by the person
who bears the name. So to pray in the name of Jesus is to pray
as he prayed, with complete trust and obedience. Such prayer
cannot be selfish, cannot be centered on material blessings
for narrow temporal ends. It is Jesus who has taught the
world, as no one else has done, what true prayer is. His was a
fellowship with the Father, full of humility, trust, forgiveness,
passionate longing, and consecrated zeal for the eternal well-
being of men. Anything asked in his name receives its
answer. But if we would understand these words, let us
remember the cross to which the consecrated prayer of Jesus

took him. Such prayer is also love as the next verse (15) shows. To pray in the name of Jesus is to love him and to love him is to follow him in thought, word, and deed.

In the Johannine tradition the sayings about asking in Jesus' name are unconditional. The conditions found elsewhere in the New Testament are surely implicit in Johannine teaching, and may have been dictated by the realistic experience in the life of the community that not all requests are granted. Some of these conditions are: keeping the commandments (1 Jn 3:22), asking according to God's will (1 Jn 5:14), having agreement of several Christians on what should be asked, and believing (Mt 18:19, 21:22), and, finally, being in charity with one's neighbor (Mt 6:14).

The phrases "in my name" and "I will do" indicate the belief that Jesus and the Father are so related (Jn 14:9-10) that petitionary prayer may be directed to the Son. In 15:16 the efficacy of prayer in Jesus' name is presented as a product of the close union with Jesus to which the disciples have been called. In 16:23-26 John completes his teaching on prayer in his name. It is a form of prayer which arises from Jesus' glorification and the gift of the Spirit (16:13-14); it is heard because of the intimacy between the Father and the believer.

Jesus promises the coming of the Paraclete (14:15-17). The essential point to grasp is that the picture of the future which this discourse paints, leaves an important gap which John fills with his doctrine on the Paraclete. Jesus is the way to the Father and also the revelation of the Father. But he is withdrawn from the disciples' sight. They will perform his mission with security, because of the mutual indwelling which unites them with him. He will no longer be their visible teacher and guide. But primitive Christianity had a vivid sense of possession of the Holy Spirit maintaining the life of the Church in the interval before the Parousia. This is an experience which overcomes the difficulty of the absentee Lord. There is still an identifiable divine presence when the visible presence of Jesus is withdrawn.

"I will pray the Father and he will give you another Paraclete, to be with you forever, the Spirit of truth. . . He will dwell with you and will be in you" (14:16-17). The parallel between the Spirit's work for the disciples and Christ's, brings out powerfully the personal character of the Spirit. Note also throughout these two verses the definite personality of the Spirit, distinct from the Father who gives him and from the Son who promises him. Note also the three prepositions: the Paraclete is with us for fellowship; he abides by our side to defend us; he is in us as a source of power to each individually, as an inward principle sanctifying, inspiring, guiding, and filling us with peace and joy.

The basic functions of the Paraclete are twofold: he comes to the disciples and dwells within them, guiding them and teaching them about Jesus; but he is hostile to the world and puts it on trial. The Paraclete is the Spirit who operates in the Christian proclamation of the redemption effected in Jesus the Messiah, and thus confirms and instructs the Church and pricks the conscience of the world. The age of the Church is the era of the Spirit to whom is attributed the divine presence in sanctification and testimony throughout the Church's life. And the gift of the Spirit is given without limits of time, and assures forever communion with Christ who sends him.

The Paraclete is the Spirit of truth whose reasonings fall dead on the ears of the world and are taken in only by the faithful. In 14:26 he is to teach and remind them. In 15:26 he is to bear witness to Christ. In 16:7-11 he is to convince or convict the world. In short, he is presented as one who suggests true reasonings to our minds and true courses for our lives, convicts our adversary, the world of wrong, and pleads our cause before God our Father. Their present Paraclete has come to them and will leave them again; the other will come and never leave them. And in him, who is the Spirit of Christ (Rm 8:9), Christ also will be with them (Mt 28:20).

The Holy Spirit is Christ's representative on earth, carrying on his work, and inspiring and strengthening his disciples to fulfill their vocation. He pleads Christ's cause in our hearts and appeals also to the better conscience of the world. He inspires believers with the spirit of prayer (Rm 8:26-27). We are to resign ourselves with implicit confidence to his guidance, for he is the Spirit of truth. He guides not so much as an external authority, as an inward light shining in the heart, an interior monitor regulating the secret springs of character. The functions of the Paraclete attest sufficiently his divinity.

"Another Paraclete" suggests evidently Jesus as the first Paraclete. In 1 Jn 2:2 Jesus is a Paraclete in the sense of heavenly intercessor in the Father's presence after the resurrection; yet John's gospel would seem to suggest that Jesus has been a Paraclete all through his earthly ministry. The Johannine term Paraclete, derived from Greek legal terminology, is used secularly for a defense attorney, a spokesman, an intercessor, although none of these terms fits precisely in John. The Paraclete in John is a teacher, a witness to Jesus, and a prosecutor of the World. He represents on earth the continued presence of the Jesus who has returned to the Father. The Paraclete comes as Christ's other self not so much to supply for his absence as to confirm his presence.

Christ is a Paraclete because he is represented as transacting the concern of our souls with God (1 Jn 2:1); and for this cause he tells us, he goes to the Father (14:12). The Holy Spirit is another Paraclete because he transacts the cause of God and Christ with us, explains to us the nature and importance of the great atonement, shows the necessity of it, counsels us to receive it, instructs us how to lay hold on it, vindicates our claim to it, and makes intercession in us with unutterable groanings. As Christ acted with his disciples while he sojourned with them, so the Holy Spirit acts with those who believe in his name. The office of the Holy Spirit will continue among men till the end of time, teaching, comforting, advising, defending, and interceding for us. The Spirit of truth is a Paraclete precisely because he carries on the earthly work of Jesus. The Paraclete/Spirit differs from Jesus the Paraclete in that the Spirit is not corporeally visible and his presence is only by indwelling in the disciples. The Old

Testament theme of "God with us" is now realized in the Paraclete/Spirit who remains with the disciples forever.

The Paraclete, the Spirit of truth, reveals and inspires the true worship of God, as opposed to the prince of this world who is the father of lies (8:44). The world does not know the Spirit, because the Spirit and the things of the Spirit must be "spiritually discerned" (1 Cor 2:14). The world may have intelligence, scientific investigation, criticism, learning; but not by these means is the Spirit of truth contemplated and recognized; rather by humility, self-investigation, faith, and love.

4

THE INDWELLING OF THE TRINITY

The Paraclete (Jn 14:15-17), Jesus (18-21), and the Father (23-24) will come to dwell with those who love Jesus, bringing them great peace and joy (25-31). Jn 14:25-31 is a conclusion giving Jesus' final thoughts before departure. It is an elaboration of the gift of peace (shalom), the usual Jewish farewell.

The Paraclete (Jn 14:15-17), Jesus (18-21 and the Father (23-24) will come to dwell with those who love Jesus, bringing them great peace and joy (25-31). Having described the place which the disciples will occupy after the resurrection, as Jesus' representatives on earth (14:12-14), Jesus goes on to expound what he means by saying that he will come again and take them to himself. It will depend on the existence of a loving relationship between him and them, which will create a mutual indwelling comparable to his own relationship with the Father (21).

"I will not leave you orphans, I will come back to you" (14:18). It should be noted that John here is not concerned with the presence of Jesus' encounter by mystics; the presence of Jesus is promised, not to an ascetical elite, but to Christians in general. The language suggests primarily the return of Jesus in the resurrection apparitions, but these do not exhaust the meaning of verse (9-20). Jesus returns invisibly in the coming of the Spirit, indwelling in our hearts. There is also, of course, the coming of the great day of Christ's second advent at the Parousia.

"Yet a little while and the world will see me no more, but you will see me; because I live, and you also will live" (14:19). No longer using the allegory of the house, Jesus takes up his usual veiled way of speaking of his death, last employed in 13:33. The disciples will see Jesus because of the resurrection, but this is something in which they also share. John is introducing the reciprocal idea in view of the next verse. Evidently he wishes to guard against a view of the resurrection as if it were an event affecting only Jesus. He is anxious to show how it has a continuing effect upon the Church and upon the life of the Christian. "Because I live a life of intercession for you at the right hand of God, you shall live a life of grace and peace here below, and a life of glory hereafter."

The world has seen its last of Jesus. The disciples, however, will see him in his risen life not merely with their eyes but also with the inward, spiritual vision of faith. "You will see me" literally during the forty days, spiritually after Pentecost, when you shall enjoy communion with me so deep and satisfying that it will be better than sight. They will recognize him for what he is, the mediator between God and men, and share, through him, in his life with the Father. The world relying on its own means of knowledge will be unable to see Jesus after his death, but the disciples will experience the presence of their risen Lord ("because I live") and they will share his new life; so also will those who accept their testimony. This knowledge and participation of the life of the risen Christ prepare and anticipate what will happen at the time of the Parousia.

"On that day you will know that I am in the Father, and you in me, and I in you" (14:20). The phrase "on that day" is a prophetic formula for great divine interventions. Primarily the day of the resurrection is meant, but the sun will never set on it. Pentecost is dawning too, and by the Spirit they will understand the presence of Jesus in the Father and in them.

The phrase belongs to the vocabulary of eschatology, but the end time is anticipated in the day of Jesus' resurrection. The last days begin with the resurrection of Jesus in which the believer participates. The essential is given even now but with an open-ended perspective on the future. The phrase is applied to the realized eschatology of the Christian life. Living this life, the Christian will experience in varying degrees, depending on his sensitivity to the divine presence, the affirmation of his faith (11). The Father, the Son, and the Church share the one life. A new state of affairs now obtains, a triple mutuality of Jesus and the Father and the disciple. The mutual indwelling of Jesus and the Father and the disciples is a way of expressing the relationship, whereas the indwelling of the Spirit is a way of expressing the effect of this relationship. The relation between Jesus and his disciples reveals the nature and reality of the relation that unites Jesus and his Father.

"He who has my commandments and keeps them, he it is who loves me; and he who loves me will be loved by my Father, and I will love him and will manifest myself to him" (14:21). Christ manifests himself to us by coming with the Father to dwell in us (23-24). The Father's love for the Son will extend to the believer and draw him into the divine family. Jesus manifests himself not to the world but to his own, because he and they, together with the Father, form a circle of love and obedience, within which mutual knowledge is possible. The real basis of their union with him will not be his appearances to them, but their love for him by which their vision will constantly keep him in view. And the verification of their love must ever be in their keeping of his commands. Love is the essential condition of the mutual indwelling. To be in the Father is the same thing as to be loved by the Father, and to be in Jesus is to be the object of his love. And the consequence, to manifest himself, is practically identical with Jesus' love.

The couple, receive/keep, in the sense of knowing and putting into practice, is paralleled by the couples, hear/keep (12:47), hear/believe (5:24). Obedience is the expression of love; it lets us know concretely the love of the Father through the revelation of Christ. The condition of this shared life is love and obedience. Fellowship or communion with Christ is dependent on love which issues in obedience. It is not sufficient merely to acknowledge the law of Christ, one must also observe it in his life. Obedience is the proof of love, which in turn makes possible communion between God and man. Loving Christ and keeping his commandments are inseparable. Moreover, Christ's love for us is the basis of his self-revelation to us. Obedience is the true test of devotion; and it will be rewarded with the Father's love and the love and self-revelation of Jesus himself. Willing obedience is set forth as the road to spiritual enlightenment. Love motivates the keeping of the commandments, and indeed love is the substance of Jesus' commandments.

Judas (not Iscariot) said to Jesus: "Lord how is it that you manifest yourself to us and not to the world?" (14:22). Before Easter he does not understand that there is another mode of existence that calls for another mode of knowledge. The word "manifest" rouses Judas as the word "see" roused Philip. Both go wrong from the same cause, inability to see the spiritual meaning of Christ's words, but they go wrong in different ways. Philip wishes for a vision of the Father, a theophany, a suitable inauguration of the Messiah's kingdom. Judas supposes, with the rest of his countrymen, that the manifestation of the Messiah means a bodily appearance in glory before the whole world, to judge the Gentiles and restore the kingdom to the Jews. Judas was still looking for a Messianic theophany which would convince the world. But our Lord's promise in the Last Discourse was not for a speedy return of the Son of Man on the clouds; it was a promise of the illumination of the heart of the individual disciple. Jesus tells the disciples the true nature of the kingdom. Love, which shows itself in obedience, is the key of entrance into that kingdom. Obedience leads to spiritual union with God. Union with God brings peace. Judas feels the need for public manifestations not private revelations. Jesus answers by pointing once more to the conditions and nature of his revelation. It belongs by its very nature only to those who love the things Jesus loved, and do the things he did. It is then that they will experience that spiritual fellowship which he calls an abode or dwelling of God in the soul. This is the Christians' home away from home and brings us back to the beginning of the discourse (14:2).

"If anyone loves me, he will keep my word, and my Father will love him, and we will come to him and make our home with him" (14:23). Answering directly the question Jesus affirms that he and the Father will fix definitely their abode with those who express affectively their love by keeping his word. Thus will be realized the aspirations of the Old Testament believers. The thought of God dwelling among his people was familiar to every Jew. The united indwelling, in the heart of the individual, of the Father and the Son by means of the Spirit is purely Christian. This is a reference to the permanent abiding of the Godhead with the believer, the spiritual experience described in 1 Jn 1:3 as fellowship or communion, a key idea in Johannine theology. This divine presence can be known only by one who loves; when the Son has returned to the Father, both will come and together with the Spirit (14:16-17) make their abode with him in delightful, permanent intimacy. In Jn 6:56 the abiding is Eucharistic; in 14:2 heavenly; here mystical, requiring no qualification save sincere love of Jesus. God's dwelling with his people is completed. But the world, which does not love him or keep his words, cannot receive this manifestation.

Where the Son is, there of necessity is the Father also, as well as the Spirit, for the three are one, being different forms of the subsistence and manifestation of the same divine being. This passage illustrates the doctrine that the Persons of the Holy Trinity are inseparable and contain one another. The later technical term is perichoresis (in Greek) and circumincessio (in Latin). This manifestation is open to all who have the right dispositions for union with God. It is an interior apprehension of Jesus and the Father in the hearts of

those who love Jesus, not a mystical experience of an esoteric
kind. It is something akin to the Pauline concept of being in
Christ, a faith union maintained by grace and faith.

The Holy Spirit will interpret Christ's teaching (26) and
impart his peace (27). Jn 14:25-31 is a conclusion giving
Jesus' final thoughts before departure. It is an elaboration of
the gift of peace, the usual Jewish farewell. To go to the
Father meant Jesus' self-chosen conflict with the ruler of this
world, whose power would be broken by Christ's death and
resurrection (14:28-31). "The Paraclete, the Holy Spirit
whom the Father will send in my name, he will teach you all
things, and bring to your remembrance all that I have said to
you" (14:26). In place of the departed Christ, the faithful will
have the Spirit, as his representative and continuing his work.
He is the Paraclete who intercedes with the Father, who
pleads in human courts. He is the Spirit of truth, leading men
to the very fullness of truth (14:13), making us understand the
mysterious personality of Jesus: how he fulfills the Scriptures
(5:39), the meaning of his words (2:19) of his actions, of his
signs, of everything which the disciples had failed to
understand. In this way the Spirit is to bear witness to Christ,
and confound the incredulity of the world. The Father's
sending of the Spirit is in answer to Jesus' request and is
closely related to Christ's mission. The Father will send the
Paraclete not just instead of Jesus, but in his name, to reveal
the Son, as the Son came in the Father's name to reveal the
Father. He will teach no new truths, but the inner meaning
and hidden riches of the words and deeds of Jesus, who will
thus continue to teach the Church through his Spirit.

The disciples had shared the earthly life of Jesus and
remembered what he had said and done. The Spirit of the
risen Christ will bring them to a deeper understanding of all
this. It is thus by bringing them progressively to a better
understanding of the reality of Jesus and of the meaning of
things in relation to him, that the Spirit will teach them all
things. While still with them in visible and audible presence
Jesus was teaching his disciples, but much of what he said
was not understood, witness the interjections of Peter,

Thomas, Philip, and Judas Thaddeus. When he is no longer with them in bodily presence his helper, the Spirit of holiness will be their teacher. He will make clear the meaning of his words, and reveal to them all the things pertaining to the life of the Spirit of which they are to be ministers. Their minds will be quickened to see all things that matter and to remember all that is worth remembrance. The Spirit will awaken the words of Christ which lie like slumbering germs in the minds of the disciples, and cause them to germinate and bear fruit. Of this process, St. John's gospel itself is a striking example and a fulfillment of this promise.

"Peace I leave with you; my peace I give to you; not as the world gives do I give to you" (14:27). Peace is the customary Jewish greeting and farewell; it means soundness of body but came to be used of perfect happiness and of the deliverance brought by the Messiah. All this is given by Jesus. Christ's shalom is a gift of salvation and not merely a conventional word of farewell as it is among men. In John peace is always related to the person of Jesus and to his presence. Peace is an expression of the harmony and communion with God that was the seal of the old covenant (Nb 6:26). Hence the word came to have an eschatological and Messianic meaning (Is 9:6) virtually the same as salvation. Peace is the perfect Messianic gift: love of God and of each other, individual and collective hope, harmony, happiness. It is the spiritual tranquillity that Christ gives, which has no resemblance to what the world gives. Because Christ is this gift that he gives, Ep 2:14 can call him our peace.

It is a peace that is completely unparalleled in the world. The antithesis between Christ's way and the world's way is a frequent theme of this Last Discourse. The world gives from interested motives, because it has received or hopes to receive as much in return (Lk 6:33-34); it gives to friends and withholds from enemies (Mt 5:43); it gives what costs it nothing or what it cannot keep, as in the case of legacies; it pretends to give what is not its own, especially when it says, *"Peace, Peace,"* where there is no peace (Jr 6:14). The manner of Christ's giving is the very opposite of this. He gives what is his own, what he might have kept, what has cost him a life of suffering and a cruel death to bestow, what is open to friend and foe alike, who have nothing of their own to give in return.

Christ's peace is the peace of reconciliation with God through his death on the cross. It is not earthly joy and prosperity; it is the removal of all elements of discord from the soul. It brings comfort and strength in the midst of distress. It is the peace of courage ready to face all dangers. As a valediction it is a bestowal of blessing, and so conveys a certain power which can remain with the disciples. In the light of the foregoing discourse, Jesus' blessing carries with it the whole positive content of the abiding effects of the resurrection which he has described.

On the basis of what he has suggested about his glorification through his resurrection, Jesus again takes up the metaphor of his departure and return, and tells us that our reaction should be one of joy, because his departure completes his earthly assignment from the Father. Though the Son is equal to the Father, his glory is for the moment veiled; his return to the Father will reveal it again. "You heard me say to you, I go away, and I will return to you. If you loved me, you would rejoice because I go to the Father; for the Father is greater than I" (14:28). This last phrase cannot be isolated from the immediate context of Johannine thought. There is no question of the relations which unite the Father and the Son in perfect unity and equality (5:19-30, 10:30), but of the state of humiliation of the Son which will be changed to glorification by the Father, a glorification which is the source of spiritual benefits for the disciples. This statement is soteriological. Though Christ is one with the Father, as the Son of Man he has been sent by the Father to do his will and in this relationship the Father is greater. It does not deny equality in Trinity. In the context Jesus is in the humiliation of the flesh; the return to the Father will be a return to the glory of the Son of God. He is going from the humiliation of his earthly ministry to the glory of the Father.

Christ's departure will take place in the faith-shaking

events of the crucifixion; but the disciples are forewarned. The crucifixion is engineered by the devil and he will seem to win a victory; but what appears to be his victory is in fact his defeat. The sayings of Jesus seen in the light of current events will lead the apostles to an increase of faith (14:29). The world and its ruler has no hold whatsoever on Jesus. His Passion is due solely to a completely free act which expresses, by his perfect obedience, his love for the Father (14:30). "I do as the Father has commanded me, so that the world may know that I love the Father" (14:31). This is the only passage in the New Testament that states that Jesus loves the Father. His love consists in doing what the Father has commanded, just as the Christian's love consists in doing what Jesus has commanded.

5

THE TRUE VINE

*The allegory of the vine illustrates the disciples'
union with Christ, which is not only the condition of
bearing fruit, but actually demands it. The teaching
of the passage is primarily one of love and faith, but
it seems likely that the piece has also Eucharistic
overtones.*

Apart from the insertion of the verses on the Paraclete, Ch 14
has been a consistent and orderly treatment of the theme of
the departure of Jesus. Chapters 15 and 16 give a less unified
impression. They seem to have been composed from a variety
of homiletic pieces which John has preached on different
occasions, and now brings together to further the exposition
of 13:31-38: namely, the life of the disciples and their
encounter with the world after Jesus shall have departed. Ch
15 and 16 deal with Christ and his Church. They handle more
fully themes treated above, especially the relation of the
disciples to Christ after the resurrection, and the work of the
Holy Spirit. More definitely than in Ch 14, we look into the
future, since we deal with the internal life of the Church, the
treatment Christians may expect from the world, and the
Church's dependence on the historic revelation, as interpreted by the Spirit of truth.

　　Three dimensions are set forth in Ch 15: the believer's
relation to Christ, abiding (1-11); the relation of believer's to

one another, love (12-17); the believer's relation to the world,
separation (18-27). The chapter deals with the disciples'
union with Christ, illustrated by the allegory of the vine (1-11);
then union with one another in him (12-17); finally, the hatred
of the world to both him and them (18-27). Our Lord gives his
disciples ground for reassurance. His love and his joy will be
theirs, if they abide in him and in love for one another. For he
is the vine, the life of all the branches, if they abide in him;
they are his friends and he is laying down his life for them; he
has told them the full truth; they must not expect to be better
treated than their Master, whose message was rejected by
those who have not known him or his Father. The Spirit will
come to help them, and they must be his witnesses.

As the true vine, Jesus is the true Israel, fulfilling the
vocation in which the old Israel had failed. The fruit bearing of
the new Israel, the Church, springs from union, actual
incorporation with Christ (5) through prayer (7), and loving
obedience (9-10), issuing in joy (11). The theme of the allegory
is the relation of the Christian to Christ, the community of life
they share, and Christ's life as the source of the good works of
Christians. The figure of the vine and the branches presup-
poses that the Christian life is essentially one of activity, of
bearing fruit; union with Christ is not only the condition of
bearing fruit, it actually demands it.

The Old Testament supplied the raw material from which
John composed the allegory of the vine. The idea of Israel as a
vine, chosen and afterwards rejected is well-known in the Old
Testament, especially in Is 5:1-3. Later Jesus gives it a new
emphasis in the parable of the wicked husbandmen (Mt
21:33-44). In the Synoptics he uses the vine as the symbol of
the kingdom of God and the fruit of the vine becomes the
Eucharistic sacrament of the New Covenant. Here he unfolds
the mystery of the true vine. He calls himself the true vine
whose fruit, the true Israel, will not disappoint God's
expectations. If the Sitz im Leben (life situation) of the allegory
of the vine is the Eucharistic assembly, it may be a sustained
metaphor based on the Eucharistic words of Jesus. It is
communion in the one cup which lays upon the disciples the

obligation of mutual love. Now this is precisely the idea which Jesus is expounding in the allegory of the vine.

The vine was one of the commonest objects in Palestine. The terraced hillsides show that the vine once flourished everywhere. The one important thing in the figure is the relation of the branches to the vine. There are many branches, but only one life. That is a common teaching of the New Testament. Personality remains, individuality remains: I am I, he is he, and you are you. But across the gulf of the individual consciousness which parts us from one another, Jesus Christ assumes the divine prerogative of passing and joining himself to each of us, if we love him and trust him, in a union so close and a communion of life so real that every other union which we know is but a faint and far-off adumbration of it.

The image of the vine was often applied to the people of Israel to indicate the love and election of which they were the object; planted and protected by God, it ought to have produced fruits of justice and holiness. According as it does not respond to God's expectation, this vine is menaced with destruction. John develops this image. Jesus is the true vine; the disciples are vitally united to him by faith and must produce works of charity. The Johannine use of the figure includes all the Old Testament associations of God's care and judgment on the vine, but at the same time it goes beyond them by its identification of Jesus as the true vine. The allegory is comparable to his discourse on the bread of life (Ch 6) and the good shepherd (Ch 10). It is another revelation of "I am." It is also a Johannine commentary on the "fruit of the vine" (Mk 14:25), the cup of the Eucharist.

The allegory is perlucid; it strikingly illustrates the community of life shared by Christ and the Christians, as well as the dynamic quality which is the character of this life: it produces fruit. This living unity results in oneness of relation between God and men, in oneness of character, and oneness of destiny. In the first we receive the standing of sons, which determines our relation to one another; in the second, we are sharers in his righteousness; in the third we are to be where he is. The figure of the vine in John invites comparison with

Pauline doctrine of Christ, the head of his body, the Church. The Pauline idea, however is far more developed; though St. John's gospel was finished long after the Pauline epistles, John is faithful to the historical age in which the gospel is set and therefore does not develop the application given it by Jesus.

In the Bible Israel is spoken of as a vineyard (Is 5:1-7, Mt 21:33-46) and as a vine (Jr 2:21). Wisdom (Si 24:17) also describes herself as a vine. All this is important background for Jesus' use of this figure as a self-description. In the Synoptic description of the Eucharist at the Last Supper we hear of "the fruit of the vine." The Didache refers to the Eucharistic cup as "the holy vine of David your servant, revealed through Jesus Christ." Consequently, there must be an implicit Eucharistic symbolism here in St. John. This is an allegory about the intimate union of love between Jesus and his own, permeated with the Eucharistic spirit and closely resembling Ch 6. The Father, who gives the bread of life (6:32) is here the vinedresser. The fidelity in faith and confidence insisted on in Ch 14 has deepened into a communion of life with Jesus and one another, bearing its fruit in love, which, like the Eucharist, is an epitome of the Christian religion.

The figure of the vine must have been suggested to Jesus by the Supper of which they had partaken. They had drunk a cup from the vine, emblem of the outpouring of his life in sacrificial love. Often as they had walked to the Mt. of Olives, they had seen vines carved upon its gates, symbols of the true Israel. The vine appeared on Maccabean coins as the emblem of the nation. The metaphor was then one very familiar both to Jesus and the disciples. Jesus had frequently used it in his teaching. There is, however, a peculiar appropriateness in the message it conveys to the disciples during the last hours they had with him in the flesh. It is a declaration of the condition, and the need of fruitfulness. If the key to Ch 14 is peace, the key to Ch 15 is fruitfulness.

The figure of the vine and the branches corresponds to that of the body and the members, used first by Christ at the institution of the Holy Supper (Mt 26:26), and often afterwards by St. Paul, to express the mysterious but real and vital union between Christ and individual believers, and between Christ and his Church. As the vine sends sap into every branch, causing the grapes to grow and ripen, so Christ communicates spiritual life and grace to every soul that is effectively in him, causing it to bring forth the fruit of the Spirit (Gal 5:22), to be fruitful in every good work (Col 1:10) and, the greatest gift of all, to be partakers of the divine nature (2 P 1:4). Union with Christ is normally begun in baptism (1 Cor 12:13), and maintained by constant faith (Ep 3:17), obedience (Jn 14:23), love (Jn 4:12), and the holy Eucharist (Jn 6:56).

The metaphor of the vine was apparently suggested by "the fruit of the vine" which had just been consecrated in the Holy Supper (Mt 26:29), and the allegory was intended to illustrate the main idea underlying that holy rite, namely, union with Christ. It sets forth Christ as the sole source of spiritual life, and of Christian sanctity. As long as the spiritual union between Christ and the believer, which ideally and normally, begins with baptism, is maintained by faith, love and prayer, the believer's soul is nourished by constant supplies of grace, just as truly as the branches of a vine are nourished by the sap that flows into them from the stem. Nourished by the life of Christ, the believer's soul is cleansed, sanctified, and made fruitful in all good works. Neglect of prayer, the holy sacraments and the other means of grace is punished by interruption of this union, and finally, by its complete severance, resulting in spiritual death, and inability to perform works acceptable to God.

The basic meaning of the vine is quite clear. Just as Jesus is the source of living water and is the bread from heaven that gives life, so he is the life-giving vine. Hitherto the metaphors that concern the receiving of Jesus' gift of life have involved external actions: one has had to drink the water or eat the bread to have life. The imagery of the vine is more intimate, as befits the general theme of interiorization in the Last Discourse: one must remain in Jesus as a branch remains on a vine in order to have life. Drinking water and eating bread are symbols of believing in Jesus; the explanation in 15:7-17 makes it clear that remaining on the vine is symbolic of love. It then seems likely that the allegory of the vine and branches has Eucharistic overtones. The teaching of the piece is primarily one of love and faith. But the narrative must have served in Johannine circles the paraenetic purpose of insisting that Eucharistic union must last and bear fruit, and must deepen the union between Jesus and his disciples already existing through love.

"I am the true vine, and my Father is the vinedresser" (15:1). In John, the great "I am" saying reveals Jesus' divine being usually as source of salvation. It is he who by the shedding of his blood (the fruit of the vine) makes possible the existence of the true people of God, whose members are what they are in virtue not of their physical descent but of their abiding in him. As often in John, the Christological term draws attention rather to the work than to the essential status of Christ. The Father as vinedresser stands over the whole process, directing its outcome; Christ is the means by which men are related to God. Whatever figure Jesus used to express his salvific work, he characterizes himself as the instrument of the Father.

The most prominent symbols of Israel in the Old Testament are the palm tree, the olive tree, and the vine. In Ps 80, God's people is compared to a vine God brought out of Egypt and is even called the Son of Man. All that Israel was destined to be, but failed to be, Jesus was, the ideal vine, producing acceptable fruit for God in his personal life and in the lives of his disciples, united to him by faith. Christ is the true, genuine, ideal, perfect vine, as he is the perfect light, bread, and witness. The material creations of God are only inferior examples of that finer spiritual life and organism in which the creature is raised up to partake of the divine nature.

Using the language of vine-growers, Jesus describes that living union between himself and his disciples on which rests the future of the new fellowship he is founding. Jesus, the Father's perfect planting (Mt 15:13) is here the total Christ, one with his disciples. The main thought behind the metaphor is that of the one source of spiritual life among men.

Humanity should be as a vine, of which the life incarnate in Christ is the vitalizing unity. Men are not isolated sticks, but branches deriving their true life from the one vine stock, out of which they spring. The metaphor is one expressive of the true unity purposed by God for the human race in that life incarnate in the Son.

"Every branch of mine that bears no fruit, he takes away, and every branch that does bear fruit he prunes, that it may bear more fruit" (15:2). The purpose of any vine is to bear fruit, hence the vine cannot be considered apart from its fruit-bearing branches. The fruit of Christ's vine is that of a life of obedience to the commandments, especially that of love. To be in Christ is basic for Christian life and for fruitfulness in that love of each other which is the essence of discipleship. The branch shares the life of the stock to which it is attached; so also the believer by adherence to Christ participates in the real life which is that of God. This participation imposes the obligation of living and acting according to Christ's new revelation.

A good dresser looks at the usefulness of each branch. A completely fruitless branch is not worthy of a place in the vine, while pruning can improve branches with a poor yield. Among the disciples, Judas proved no true part of the vine, while all others underwent pruning experiences before producing much fruit at Pentecost. Pruning refers also to the discipline of sorrow, disappointment, temptation, and trial by which believers are perfected; to the cutting off of superfluities, ambitions, luxuries, and worldly pleasures and lusts, which hinder the Christian life.

"You are already made clean by the word which I have spoken to you" (15:3). Christian purification is effected essentially by faith in the word or teaching of Jesus, who presents God's saving plan for mankind. The point of purification is not stressed here; Jesus is focusing on the fruitfulness of the Christian life, although he will show himself quite severe for those who refuse to abide in him (6).

"Abide in me, and I in you. As the branch cannot bear fruit by itself, unless it abides in the vine, neither can you, unless you abide in me" (15:4). This is the pith and point, the heart not only of the parable but of Christianity itself. Everything depends on our maintaining a living union with our Lord. From this springs all depth of devotion, all effective Christian service. The two clauses "abide in me" and "I in you" constitute at once the condition and the source of Christian fruitfulness. For man to abide in Christ is to retain firmly and actively what has been given in the past, hold it in the present, and face the future in function of it. It is also in this sense that the believer abides in the word (8:31), in love (15:9-10), in the light (1 Jn 2:10), in God (1 Jn 4:13-16). On the other hand, for God or for Christ to abide expresses the stability of the gifts of salvation accorded to believers (1 Jn 2:27). Remaining in Jesus and having Jesus remain in the disciple are parts of the whole, for there is only one personal relationship between Jesus and his disciples; if they remain in Jesus through faith, he remains in them through love and faithfulness.

"He who abides in me, and I in him, he it is who bears much fruit, for apart from me you can do nothing" (15:5). Christ is the whole vine not only the stem. The disciples as branches are part of him, and to be effective, must completely depend on him. Without denying the reality and proper value of human enterprises, it must be recognized that they ultimately face a vacuum, if those who accomplish them have not established themselves in communion with Christ, who alone can confer on them an eternal value. "If you abide in me, and my words abide in you, ask whatever you will, and it shall be given to you" (15:7). Fruitful prayer is defined as communion with Christ. To dwell in Christ is to have the secret of effective prayer. "By this is my father glorified, that you bear much fruit, and so prove to be my disciples" (15:8). To bear much fruit is to live the life of true discipleship and thereby glorify God. The thought moves between God's initiative in love, and man's loving obedience. The fruitfulness of his vine is the joy and glory of the vine-grower; all ends, as it began, with the Father.

6

THE PARACLETE'S WITNESS

The allegory of the vine is followed by a paraenetic development on Christian love. Believers must remain in Jesus, abide in his love (15:7-10) and love one another as Christ has loved us (12-17). The world will hate and persecute the disciples (18-25), but co-witnessing with the Holy Spirit is the mission of the Church (26-27).

The allegory of the vine is followed by a paraenetic development on Christian love. Believers must remain in Jesus, abide in his love (7-10) and love one another as Christ has loved us (12-17). The world will hate and persecute the disciples (18-25), but co-witnessing with the Holy Spirit is the mission of the Church (26-27).

"As the Father has loved me, so I have loved you; abide in my love" (15:9) The vine growing images shade away into the plain language of love. The measure of the Father's love for the Son is the measure of Christ's love for his disciples. Let them stay on in the shelter of his love for them; and the secret of such continuance is obedience to his commands, summed up in the sovereign one of a self-giving love like Christ's own. The obedient love of Jesus for his Father, to which corresponds the love of the Father glorifying his Son, constitutes the basis and eminent model for Christian living which consequently is expressed in Christian love.

Christian fellowship is grounded in the eternal love of the Father which Jesus knew. Of this originating love, he has been the channel to them. Let them then abide therein. The spirit of obedience to him will secure this permanent union; as his own obedience to the Father has secured it for himself. Love and obedience are therefore correlatives. While the eternal love of the Father is the ground of all true fellowship, our human obedience is the condition of its continuance. Such obedience is both the way to eternal life and one of its essential constituents.

"If you keep my commandments, you will abide in my love, just as I have kept my Father's commandments and abide in his love" (15:10). The love which is a response to Christ's love is expressed concretely with a fruitfulness which follows from the observance of the commandments, briefly, the commandment of fraternal love. Christian love is not merely a question of unity of will existing in virtue of an affective relationship, but a unity of being by virtue of a divine quality. For John love is related to being or remaining in Jesus. This loving relationship of mutual indwelling is pre-eminently a moral union. Hence love is shown by the voluntary keeping of the Master's commandments. Above the vine stands the husbandman. Here, as always, it is the Father's will that is done. There is no room in this vine for branches which have merely a nominal connection. Love is not complacency: it is care. The same love destroys the unprofitable servant and exalts the loyal disciple. The Father is glorified in the fruitfulness of the disciple. This is possible if the disciple abides in his Lord's love, as Jesus abides in the Father's love.

"These things I have spoken to you that my joy may be in you, and that your joy may be full" (15:11). The obedience and love to which Jesus calls his disciples both constitute and witness their union with him; and it is this union that will be the source of their joy, the perfect happiness of the Messianic era which is communicated by the Son of God. Nothing causes so much joy as to be loved, and Jesus desires to enlarge their hearts by the fullness of joy; the delightful divine merriment of the Christians, which originates in the Son and is deposited in his disciples, is matured and perfected as they love one another, undergo persecution, and readily lay down their lives for their brethren. Joy, the sign of a flourishing life, was considered in the Old Testament, as the characteristic of the time of salvation and of eschatological peace. The theme reappears in the gospels. In John, the joy of the risen Christ is shared, even now, by the disciples who live the new life. This joy must possess the whole person and reach some sort of plenitude. It can actually coexist with suffering.

Love can subsist only if it produces more love. Notice the chain found in 15:9-12: the Father loves Jesus; Jesus loves the disciples who, in turn, must love one another. Only the love of God for us and our love to him can satisfy the deepest desires of our being. Jn 15:12-17 deals with the relation of believers to one another, namely, love. The measure is determined by Jesus' death (13). Fellowship with Jesus (14-15), fruit bearing and prayer (16), are all dependent on obeying his command to love (17).

"This is my commandment that you love one another as I have loved you" (15:12). Christian love has as its model nothing less than the example of the Good Shepherd himself; in turn the love of Christ gives the Christian the ability to live up to this ideal. The disciples are to love one another (12, 13, 17); not because John thinks it unnecessary that Christians should love their enemies (Mt 5:44), but because the mutual love of Christians is in a peculiar way related to the mutual love between the divine Persons.

"Greater love than this no man has, that a man lay down his life for his friends" (15:13). Our Savior now resolves his commands into perfect self-forgetting love. Christian love, here below, is expressed mostly in self-sacrifice. "Friends" means those whom we love. Although expressed in general terms, this is, of course, a self-portrait of Jesus himself, as the model for the mutual love of the disciples. Jesus is referring to his own approaching death, conceived as an act of sacrifice on behalf of others. The death of Jesus on the cross was the supreme expression of his love for his Father; it is also the summit of his love for those he has made his own. This is the foundation and the norm of fraternal love.

To lay down one's life for one's friends is the ultimate extension of love. Once more the newness of his command-ment of love is brought out. Only the Son of God could make such a demand which is dictated by no natural law of life, and which no other religious teacher would dare to assert on his own authority. It is such a concept of the duty of the love of neighbor that is part of the folly of the gospel (1 Cor 1:23), a folly, we must add in all honesty, of which very few Christians are prepared to be found guilty. Folly and paradox though it be, it is a law of life and death revealed in the Christ-event and thereby constituted the law of Christianity (1 Jn 3:16). Though by worldly standards it is a self-defeating principle, in fact, it has proved to be source of all life. To accept it as such, to live by its norms, requires great faith; but any faith that falls short of it is of necessity less than Christian.

Sacrifice of life for one's friends is here commended as the highest love. Some people have contrasted this saying unfavorably with Rm 5:8 where Paul says: "Christ died for us while we were yet sinners, and that is God's own proof of his love towards us." But this criticism is hardly fair for Jesus happens for the moment to be speaking to his friends of the supreme pledge of his love he is about to show them; and elsewhere (6:51) he says that his sacrifice is for the life of the world. St. Paul says that such cases of self-sacrifice for good men occur; but they are rare. Christ, however, surpassed them, for he died not only for his friends but also for his enemies, not only for the good but also for sinners.

Christ's disciples are not his servants but his friends "for all that I have heard from the Father, I have made known to you" (15:14-15). The change of relationship from servants to friends is significant because of what friends are able to share. It is strongly expressed as "all that I have heard from the Father." A slave obeys his master without being allowed to know the reason for his Lord's action. But a friend is let into his master's secrets, as Christ's disciples have been let into his, which are his heavenly Father's. The love of friendship is mutual, a love that is exchanged. We enter into God's intimate life and share it. We are introduced into familiarity with him. To remain in Christ's love can thus be seen not only as the greatest but also, in a way, as the only commandment. When we recall the great number of servants and slaves who were among the first Christians, the word gets new significance. Friends have a mutual intimacy and confidence on equal terms. Jesus has given the disciples this kind of confidence in imparting to them the full message of salvation from the Father.

"You did not choose me, but I chose you and appointed you that you should go and bear fruit, and that your fruit should abide; so that whatever you ask the Father in my name, he may give it to you" (15:16). The divine initiative is exclusively his. They are not his slaves but his chosen friends, standing within the circle of mutual knowledge and love, of which Father and Son are the coincident foci. The metaphor of fruitfulness returns once more, again in connection with prayer (16, 7). There is no really stable religious life which does not arise out of the conviction of the prevenient grace and call of God. The life that flows into the branches from the stem of the vine is the sap of humility as well as love. Christ's choice was motivated by his desire to have them as his companions (Mk 3:14), his friends, and then to send them out as his missionaries. His sending them forth is grounded in his confidence in them as friends, and this conversely is their ground of confidence in prayer. Their work has lasted for 2000 years and the vitality of Christian missionary work is still unimpaired.

Even if all friendships suppose a mutual free choice, John underlines the fact of the absolute priority of Jesus' choice. He thus takes up an important Old Testament theme, well-known in the Synoptic gospels. For John, the choice of Jesus concerning his disciples is the expression of the Father's choice. The eternal election is expressed in the vocation to which one responds by faith. The divine initiative has been paramount throughout the history of our salvation. The Son was sent by the Father, and the Son has chosen his own, whose mission and whose life, therefore, continue a work of divine grace.

The commission with which the disciples have been invested by their Lord supposes the assurance of the means to exercise the function effectively. The purpose of the mission is to have men participate in the eternal life offered in Jesus. Confident prayer, calling on Jesus for help, is an essential aspect of his friendship and of their mission. Apostolic effectiveness depends on it radically. The efficacy of prayer in Christ's name is presented as the product of the close union with Jesus to which the disciples have been called. Finally, the vine image finds its key and its close, and all its teaching summed up by the mutual love modeled on Christ's love. "This I command you, to love one another" (15:17). Both here and in verse 12, love is said to be a command, which shows its essential character.

The key word now passes from love to hate (15:18-21). In contrast with the disciples' love for one another, Jesus warns them that their relation to the world will be different. In this also they will be only sharing his experience. Jesus loves his disciples because they remain or abide in him; the world hates them for the same reason. Men hate Jesus primarily because of what they themselves are. His goodness rouses to fury the evil that is in them. The first principle is the essential hatred of the world. Hate is the antithesis of love and involves hostility. The second principle is that in spiritual matters, like attracts like and repeals opposites. Hate is as much of the essence of the world as love is of the essence of Christianity. The world is often an ambivalent word, here it indicates Jesus' enemies. There is no warrant here, however, for an otherworldly outlook, as if Christ's disciples are to contract out of involvement in the ordinary affairs of men. But by our incorporation into Christ, we form a distinct category in society. The believer's relation to the world consists in separation (15:18-25) and bearing witness to Christ in the power of the Holy Spirit (26-27); this will involve persecution (16:1-4).

3

The mission of the disciples is continuous with that of Jesus himself. The world can only love its own, but the Christians are Christ's, so that the world's hatred of them is simply the continuation, or further expression, of its hatred of Christ whom it hates precisely because he stands over against it, bearing witness to its sin, and demonstrating a kind of life, and in a particular a kind of love, which is diametrically opposed to its own. Because they are vitally united to Jesus, the disciples will share the persecution and hatred the world shows to Jesus; the antagonism between God and the world constitutes an essential aspect of salvation history. No one can escape it.

The world's hatred is due to the ignorance of the character of God: "Because they do not know him who sent me" (15:21). The sin, par excellence, consists in refusing to accept God who manifests himself in Jesus. Unbelief is manifested by hatred. The world cannot plead ignorance, for they have seen God act in Jesus and in rejecting Jesus they have rejected God. This is what the Synoptics call the sin against the Holy Spirit (Mk 3:29-30). Jesus' coming, his words and his works, were the grace and mercy of God intended for the salvation of the world. But the ill-disposed who have loved the glory of men rather than of God, they have been the occasion of a further sin of rejecting God and Christ (Jn 15:22-24).

With the Paraclete at their side, the hatred of the world will be powerless, both over the disciples and over the truth which is their cause. For the Paraclete is the Spirit of truth, proceeding from the Father, who is the fount of truth, bearing witness to Jesus who is the incarnate expression of truth. The disciples in virtue of their fellowship with Jesus since the beginning of his public ministry, will bear the same witness (15:26-27). Christ continues to bear witness through the mission of the other Paraclete, who in turn operates continuously with the ministry of the disciples. He bears witness and they bear witness, on the basis of their long relationship with Christ. And the Paraclete proceeds from the Father who is thus the ultimate agent in witness-bearing.

This refers directly to the sending of the Spirit into the world rather than to the eternal proceeding from the Father within the Trinity. It concerns directly the role of each Person in the work of revelation.

"The Spirit of truth will bear witness to me, and you also will be witnesses, because you have been with me from the beginning" (15:26). Proceeding from the Father, the Spirit is sent by the glorified Christ to whom he is intimately united. The Spirit bears witness of the Spirit of truth, who has the authority of the Father; it is impossible to have higher witness than this. According to 14:17 it is the Father who sends the Spirit; now it is Christ himself, showing clearly that "whatever the Father does the Son does likewise" (Jn 5:19).

This witness of the disciples is not different or distinct from that of the Paraclete; rather it exteriorizes the Paraclete's internal witness. Those sent to witness have shared the life of Jesus from the beginning of his ministry, but their witness is also the work of the Spirit of truth who assures the deep intelligence of the mind of Christ, and who thus gives to the preaching of the disciples its true power and truth. Co-witnesses of the Holy Spirit, such is the calling of Christ's disciples, now as then. Jesus is the supreme revelation of God to men; there can be no witness to the world other than the witness he bore. All other witness by the Paraclete through the disciples simply interprets that.

Christ's disciples by living the life he has made possible, by being the Church, the continuation of Christ in the world, will be a continuing witness to his work. This is, indeed, at the same time the witness of the Spirit, since it is the Spirit sent by the Son from the Father who will be the soul of the Church. We, of the present day, first livingly experience, through the New Testament Scriptures, the life, deeds, and sayings of our Lord, as eye and ear witnesses of the second degree; then we also wait humbly for the power from on high; then it is our obligation and right to testify with power to what we have seen and heard in historical conviction and living experience.

7

THE CONDEMNATION OF THE WORLD

When the Spirit comes, he will convince the world of sin and of righteousness and of judgment (Jn 16:8).

In Ch 16 the thoughts of the previous chapters recur, like the themes in the several movements of a symphony. We have been told that the separation of the Church from the world is a matter not of social but of theological significance. The world's attitude to the Church arises out of and affects its attitude towards God; its condemnation of the Church means its own judgment by God. The theme of judgment is more developed, not as in the synoptic apocalypses, in an account of what will take place at the end of world history, but in a description of the work of the Paraclete in the life and experience of the Church.

The disciples must expect excommunication and persecution but they will have this forewarning to help them (16:1-4); and they need not grieve too much that Jesus is leaving them; that is necessary that he may send them his Spirit (5-7) who will both plead their cause before the eyes of the world (8-11) and will teach them more of the Father's mind about future things, which will be his own teaching too (12-15). Jesus must go and they will grieve but their grief will soon be turned into joy; they will see him again; he will teach them more plainly still, and his Father will answer all prayers offered in his name (16-24). They have put faith in him as having come from the Father; true in spite of that, they may desert him for a while, but ultimately they will have peace in the assurance of his own victory over the world (25-33).

The difficulties which the hatred of the world will provoke against Jesus and his disciples, will surely exercise their faith. When these experiences come to the disciples, they will remember how this opposition of darkness to light, of falsehood to truth was the burden of Christ's closing message. To know these things in advance will be a source of strength and comfort to those who suffer; they will know that their Master has not been surprised by opposition, and that their sufferings have a place in the fulfillment of his purpose. To be forewarned is to be forearmed.

So far John has been concerned with the way the disciples are to behave in the future, abiding in Jesus' love (15:1-17) and ready to face persecution (15:18-16:4). Now he turns to the necessity of Jesus' departure which was the major concern in Ch 14. For this purpose he uses two distinct kinds of material, on the work of the Paraclete (16:7-15), and on the joy of the new relation which will be established (16-24). There will be a full-scale exposure of the world, presumably through the disciples' preaching (8-11) and a comprehensive instruction of their minds (12-15).

The perspective of Jesus' departure saddens the disciples to the point of stifling every other thought. They will overcome this sadness when they really grasp the meaning of Christ's departure and understand that it is passing into glory and the origin of the gift of the Spirit. The glorification of Christ's humanity through the indwelling Spirit was not complete till the resurrection and ascension, hence not till after the ascension could the Spirit of the glorified Christ be given.

"It is to your advantage that I go away, for if I do not go away, the Paraclete will not come to you; but if I go, I will send him to you" (16:7). There is a twofold point in these words. First the departure of Christ in the body is both the necessary condition and the cause of future individual union. Then each

member of Christ's spiritual body will be a veritable shrine of
deity. Second, it will be to the disciples' advantage that the
Spirit, when he is imparted, will empower the Church's
ministry convicting the world of its state before God. The work
of the Spirit will be through the Church. Sorrow at Jesus'
departure is transformed by the truth that his death and
resurrection make possible the Spirit's work. The work of the
Spirit depended on the completion of the work of Christ. But
more, through the work of the Spirit, Jesus will take a larger
place in history than was possible while he was still in the
world. The conception of the fourth gospel is that the death of
Jesus means the breaking down of those limitations of space
and time and power which were necessarily involved in
Christ's earthly life.

   We sometimes envy those who were with Jesus on
earth. Yet when the crisis came, the faith which relied on
external presence went to pieces. A few weeks later, and
these same faithless disciples exhibited a strange new
boldness and joy in the teeth of persecution. What explains
the change? Jesus' promise had come true. It was better for
them that Christ's personal presence should be withdrawn, in
order that his spiritual presence might be nearer to them than
ever, or rather, might for the first time truly begin. This would
be effected by the Holy Spirit when he who was with them
would be ever in them. There is no suggestion that Jesus and
the Spirit cannot be present to the disciples at one and the
same time, but of one era, one mission coming after the other
one. The departure of Jesus, that is, his death, must be
accepted by the disciples as an essential element of their
response of faith, if they are to be capable of receiving the
Spirit. And John conceives the chief function of the Spirit, to
be producing in the disciples the works which Jesus has done
in his incarnate life.

   Jn 16:8-11 illustrates the Paraclete's condemnation of
the world. The Spirit will convince the world that unbelief in
Jesus is sin (9), that the cross reveals God's righteousness
(10), and brings judgment by triumphing over evil (11). As the
one who represents the risen Christ, the Paraclete is here

assigned a threefold task: to pass judgment on the sin of the world, to testify to Jesus' presence with the Father, and to attest to God's condemnation of the powers of evil. Think of a trial bearing on the guilt of one party and the innocence of the other and ending with a condemnation. The Spirit's witness, ringing through the kerygma, will reveal the true meaning of Jesus' death. The Holy Spirit through the apostolic preaching, and through the new power of holiness manifested in the lives of believers, will convince mankind of their sin and folly in rejecting Christ; that Christ is a sincere and righteous teacher, and not, as they had thought an impostor, as will be clearly demonstrated when the Father raised him from the dead and set him at his right hand in heaven. The Spirit will convict the world of sin, as a fact in itself; of righteousness, as a fact in Christ; and of judgment, condemnation, as a fact in the ruler of this world.

The Paraclete will convince the world of sin, because the sin of the world has been completely manifested in its failure to believe in Jesus; here its egocentricity became perfectly manifest in its rejection of God and assertion of itself. The departure of Jesus to the Father means his crucifixion and resurrection, and this twofold event means at once the offering of a perfectly obedient life and the ratification of that life by God's acceptance of the offering. And what appeared to be the condemnation of Jesus was, by God's act in the resurrection, turned into the condemnation of his accusers. The sequence sin, righteousness, and judgment is significant. The Spirit will show that men are sinners because of their unbelief in Christ; that Jesus is righteous and has been vindicated by his exaltation; and that the ruler of the world, Satan, is evil and has been judged at the cross. With this assurance of the Spirit's activity, the disciples need not fear what lay in store for them.

The courtroom is in the mind and understanding of the disciples. The trial is only indirectly the trial of the world. It is properly a rerun of the trial of Jesus in which the Paraclete makes the truth emerge for the disciples to see. Its effect on the world stems from the fact that, having been assured by the Paraclete of the victory of Jesus in that trial, the disciples go forth to bear witness (15:27) and thus challenge the world and its interpretation of the trial. In being the moving force behind this, the Paraclete is simply continuing the work of Jesus, who himself bore evidence against the world that what it does is evil (7:7).

In the fourth Gospel the concept of the Spirit as Paraclete continues and completes a pattern of prophetic witness which is one of its stresses. This witness to truth, light, and life, against falsehood, darkness, and death, the perpetual witness of the prophetic word has been the testimony of prophets like Abraham, Moses, Isaiah, and John the Baptist. It reaches its apex in the incarnation of the prophetic Word, in Jesus Christ. But now Christ about to withdraw his visible presence from the world, leaves behind the prophetic Spirit of God to continue the testimony, the Spirit of prophecy now incarnate in his Church. It is in this incarnational state, as the soul of living men, that the Holy Spirit will convict the world of sin, and of justice, and of judgment.

"He will convince the world of sin because they do not believe in me; of righteousness because I go to the Father, and you will see me no more; of judgment, because the ruler of this world is judged" (16:9-11). The world's sin is unbelief; the Spirit will expose it. The sin of the world consists first of all in refusing to believe in Jesus, in refusal of the light. The supreme sin lies in unbelief. Jesus' return to the Father will mark the vindication of his righteous life here below, and since his return to the Father is by way of resurrection, he pronounces judgment over the prince of this world whose domain is clearest in death. In this sentence is prophesied the Church's spiritual power within and over the world.

The Holy Spirit will join his testimony to that of Jesus (3:11) so that the justice of his cause may appear before the eyes of believers. The condemnation and ignominious execution of Jesus appeared to men as proof of imposture and sin, and manifested the correctness of the world's claims. But the intervention of the Spirit, by its influence on the testimony of the disciples, completely reverses this situation. By manifesting that by his death Jesus has been glorified by God, the Spirit will show the rightness of Christ's cause, and will attest unimpeachably the sin of the world and the condemnation of its ruler. The Spirit will demonstrate the right of Jesus to the title, Son of God. The passing of Jesus to the Father will prove that he is God's Son, because it will show his origin and his heavenly being. Jesus' resurrection shows that his death was not a malefactor's just punishment but a going to his Father and the vindication of his claims, proving the righteousness of his cause. The Spirit will reveal the significance of Christ's death, the defeat and condemnation of the prince of this world.

8

THE GUIDANCE OF THE DISCIPLES

The Paraclete, the Spirit of truth, will guide the disciples (Jn 16:12-15). He will lead them in all the truth. Temporary sorrow over Jesus' death will yield to joy over his resurrection and abiding presence (16-22), a joy sustained by prayer in Jesus' name (23-24). Jn 16:25-33 is a pledge of triumph. Jesus' going to the Father (28) makes plain all his teaching, reveals God's love (27), empowers prayer (26), and offers peace in tribulation (33).

The Paraclete's guidance of the disciples (Jn 16:12-15) has already been mentioned in 14:26. The Spirit not only convicts the world, he also enlightens the apostles respecting Christ, and thereby glorifies him, for to make Christ known is to glorify him. These verses are important as showing the authority of the Apostles' teaching; it is not their own, but the truth of Christ revealed by the Spirit. The Spirit as teacher will complete the apostles' education. Jesus, the Father's Word, has revealed everything to them (1:14) but the Spirit of truth will guide them into the height and depth of these riches. His guidance is sure for like the Son, he will not speak of himself. The Paraclete will bring home to men the truth of what Jesus said, not bringing out some new and independent revelation, and revealing his unity with the Father and the Son. The Spirit can guide only in harmony with his own nature, that is, truth. It is the authority of the speaker which gives importance to any statement, but the Spirit's authority is one with the Father and the Son. Christ is the way and the truth. The Spirit leads men into the way and thus to the truth. But he does no more than guide; he does not compel, he does not carry. They may refuse to follow, and if they follow they must exert themselves.

The Holy Spirit is the living source of divine revelation, and as such is the Spirit of truth. He makes truth inherent in believers, so that they grow in knowledge and grace. He bears many names: the Spirit of God, of the Father, of Christ, of the Lord, the Holy Spirit, the Spirit of wisdom, of power, of adoption, of life, the earnest of eternal life. He is the Spirit by whom truth finds expression, and is brought to man's spirit. The truth is that which the Spirit interprets and enforces. Although Jesus has transmitted to them everything he has learned from the Father (15:15), the disciples are incapable, in their actual situation to understand the full import and demands of Christ's teaching. What they must learn is their participation in the death and resurrection of Christ in virtue of the gift of the Spirit. The Lord's earthly teaching had been incomplete because it had been limited by his hearers' capacity of understanding. But the Paraclete will guide them into all the truth of Christ's gospel. The gift of the Spirit will bring the disciples to the full comprehension of the truth which is manifested integrally in the incarnate Son. Just as Christ constantly refers to the Father who sent him, so also the Spirit refers to the Son. There is no new revelation independent of that given in Jesus Christ. The Apostles' preaching and the rest of the New Testament exemplify this Spirit-taught truth.

"He will guide you into all truth." This promise is not exlusively to the Apostles; the Spirit is guiding the Church at all times in the truth, that is, in all that is necessary to the salvation of souls and to the well-being of the Church. It should be noted that the Church's apprehension of truth is regarded as progressive. "He will declare to you the things

that are to come," that is, the new order of things that is to
result from Christ's death and resurrection. The things to
come are not necessarily new future predictions. What the
Paraclete does is to make Jesus' message continually
relevant for each generation. The reference is to the whole
range of eschatological events which have been anticipated
in Jesus, and remain to be worked out through time in the life
of the Church. Prophecy as a function of the Spirit is not so
much prediction of the future, near or far, but an aspect of the
Spirit's ministry as the earnest of what is yet to be. There are
three functions of the Spirit mentioned in the Last Discourse
in which the three phases of the New Testament message
seem to be summarized, namely, history, doctrine, and
eschatology.

The Spirit will glorify Christ by leading the disciples
progressively to the knowledge of the reality manifested in
him, and, at the same time, he fulfills Christ's work which was
to glorify or manifest the Father. Thus it is that the
unbreakable unity of divine revelation appears. The glorification which the Son has from the Father and which is in turn
the glorification of the Father, is continued in the Church
through the activity of the Spirit who continues the work of
Christ. The guiding Spirit does not guide men away from
Christ, but only leads to a deeper understanding of what
Jesus said and did. There are twin centralities in Christianity:
Jesus, the Word of God Incarnate, and the Holy Spirit, the
giver of life and light. The Spirit does not usurp the authority of
the Son. But since the Son shares the authority of the Father
in revelation, the triune God is here depicted in perfect
harmony of operation.

By revealing the hidden depths of Jesus, the Spirit makes
Christ's glory known. Jesus, in his turn, manifests the glory of
the Father from whom comes everything he possesses. The
Father is the source of the revelation communicated by the
Son and brought to completion by the Spirit who in this way
glorifies both Son and Father. There are not three revelations
but one. The passage, however, is not aimed simply at
expressing the complete unity between the Father and the

Son which remains unbroken in the new situation when the Spirit is the effective agent in the furtherance of Jesus' mission. It is rather concerned with the complete identity between the mission of Jesus and the mission of the disciples under the Spirit's guidance.

Temporary sorrow over Jesus' death will yield to joy over his resurrection and abiding presence (16:16-22). This is sustained by prayer in Jesus' name, that is, his nature, all that the cross and resurrection reveal him to be (23-24). John makes a distinction between the manner of seeing Jesus during the period that is coming to a close (14:19) and that which will begin starting with his glorification. This new era will be marked by a more penetrating mode of knowing the incarnate and glorious Son. You will see me with bodily eyes during the forty days; with spiritual vision after Pentecost. "You will see me" (16:16) is a promise which includes Christ's post-resurrection appearances, his presence through the Spirit, and his second, final coming.

The disciples' intervention (16:17-19) is designed to narrow down the issue of the mysterious phrase "a little while" which recurs seven times. John is giving this phrase the greatest solemnity possible. It is equivalent in this gospel of the "after three days" in the earlier tradition. John correlates his teaching with the conventional Christian teaching of the resurrection on the third day. The death of Jesus is to John the fundamental event, for it reunites Jesus with the Father. Thus the condition of the new relationship with the disciples is fulfilled. But he can make a concession to the conventional view, in as much as the disciples only become aware of the new relationship in the resurrection experience. And this happened on the third day.

The disappearance of Jesus will provoke in his disciples a great affliction while his enemies will know the joy of triumph. This is a period in which the world will rejoice in its successful attacks upon a powerless and apparently undefended Church, a period in which the Church will experience a sorrow which the return of Christ will turn into joy. The believer's sorrow is but an avenue to true joy, which is contrasted with the world's rejoicing over the subject of the believer's lamentation over the crucifixion of Christ. Sorrow will mark the first little while, but joy will mark the second. Just as the new life given in childbirth fills the mother with joy, overcoming all the former anguish, so the joy of the resurrection, for all the world's persecution, will become the dominant factor in Christian experience.

The resurrection of Jesus will bring the disciples a joy that is as definitive as the victory of Christ. The one note expressing the situation is joy, the ineradicable joy of Jesus himself (17:13) which is to be the dynamism of the Church. The main characteristic of the joy is said to be its security. It is because the disciples' joy depends not on themselves but on Jesus, that no one can take it away from them. It rests on the reconciliation between God and man which is effected in the person of Jesus, and the visible expression of this reconciliation and communion in prayer; it follows that the Christian life will be marked by trustful, and answered prayer, and it is in this prayer that Christian joy is perfected.

Jn 16:23-26 completes his teaching on prayer in his name. It is a form of prayer which arises from Jesus' glorification and the gift of the Spirit (16:13-14). It is heard because of the intimacy between the Father and the Son. Believers will have available direct approach to God in the light of the Son's exaltation. Their anxious questions which are found heaped up in Ch 13-16 will now be replaced by the prayerful supplication they will make in Jesus' name. Until now the disciples have not prayed in his name because it is in virtue of his passage into glory that Jesus assumes fully his power of mediation (14:13). Prayer in his name, that is to say, prayer that will be addressed to Jesus as Lord of the Church, reigning over it by his Spirit as the triumphant Son of God. The disciples cannot be completely united to Jesus, and thus act in his name, until after the hour of the passion, death, and resurrection, and giving of the Spirit. Only then, as Ep 2:18 phrases it, will they have access to the Father in one Spirit.

Jn 16:25-33 is a pledge of triumph. Jesus' going to the Father (28) makes plain all his teachings, reveals God's love

(27), empowers prayer (26), and offers peace in tribulation (33). The resurrection and the coming of the Spirit will inaugurate the perfect Christian initiation which will end in the vision of God as he is (1 Jn 3:2). In particular, Jesus, through the Paraclete will tell the disciples about the Father. This is because the Paraclete comes from the Father, begets the disciples as the Father's own children, so that their knowledge of the Father is almost connatural. The real import of 16:26 is not to exclude Christ's intercession, but to explain that in interceding, Christ will not be a tertium quid between the Father and his children. Rather Jesus' necessary role in bringing men to the Father, and the Father to men, will set up so intimate a relationship of love, in and through Christ, that Jesus cannot be considered as intervening. The Father will love the disciples with the same love with which he has loved Jesus (17:23-26); and the Father, Jesus, and the disciples will be one (17:21-23). Jesus will not have to ask the Father on behalf of the Christians, for the Christian's prayer will be Jesus' prayer. In his glorified state Christ will not pray for his own; he will pray with them and through them in his Church. Here one comes to the deepest point of Christian mysticism. The Father sees in the Christians Christ himself, who is at the same time the object of their faith and love. Jesus is still the only mediator, but the disciples' faith and love make them one with him and therefore dear to the Father; the mediation of Jesus will have reached its fullest effect. Christ's mediation far surpasses that of a mere intermediary. It is fully realized in the measure in which, by a fully active faith and love, the disciples are so closely united to him that they share directly in his communion with the Father. It is in this perspective that the efficacy of prayer appears in the name (person) of Jesus.

"I came from the Father and have come into the world; again I am leaving the world and going to the Father" (16:28). This is a perfect summary of Christian faith. John embraces the whole divine scheme: the ascent proves the descent; the return the origin. Jesus explains how he is one with men and one with the Father. Coming into the world he has established a bond of union with his fellowmen; leaving the world he returns to reestablish in its fullness his union with the Father. The future relationships of the disciples to the Father result from the historic act of God in Christ. To John the incarnation and the passion are the two foci of this act. He has mentioned the incarnation in the last verse. Now he expands his words to take in the passion, using his favorite idea of Jesus' departure. He therefore brings the thought back to the actual circumstances of the setting of the discourse, which will conclude with the reader prepared for the continuation of the passion narrative.

All at once the disciples desert their somewhat studied obtuseness to take a spectacular leap into overconfidence. They naively think that they have the full understanding that is the climax of the hour of Jesus' death, resurrection and ascension (25), but the only part of the hour that is at hand for them is their share in the passion (32). In function of the Paschal event, those who had begun to believe (6:69) arrive at a deeper understanding of Jesus; they discover that Jesus possesses a perfect knowledge of events and of hearts, and that, without waiting for their questions, he brings them words which answer their expectations. This discovery leads them to a more explicit and more intense allegiance.

The confession of their faith, however, is defective because it does not include mention of Jesus' return to the Father. In fact this is the cardinal fact for the establishing of the new relationship between the disciples and the Father. The disciples have confessed faith in the deepest teaching of the discourse about the future condition, but they have failed to recognize that the crucifixion must come first. It is not then surprising that Jesus now queries their confession of faith by challenging them with their own share in the coming suffering, which is the real test of faith. The disciples unwisely presume that the hour of which Jesus has spoken is already here and that even now they possess the fullness of comprehension that he has promised. Of this presumption Jesus must disabuse them, predicting that far from being confirmed in faith, they will soon desert him in the hour of his trial, leaving him alone with his Father. "I am not alone, for the Father is with me" (16:32). Even in the darkest hour of the passion, the presence of the Father is not lacking. At every stage of his departure to the Father, the Father is with him even as at every stage of our pilgrimage to our Father's house, the Father is with us.

Jesus welcomes their faith but warns them that reciting the creed is one thing, living it, another. The apostles think that nothing could be plainer than Christ's explanation of his mission, and this before the coming of the Spirit. They base their more enthusiastic than solid faith on the correct but flimsy foundation that Jesus devines their thoughts. Their present faith is insufficient; they will not be able to resist fully to the trial of the passion. The powers of evil will disperse them and each will go his own way. It is Jesus who will reassemble them and consolidate their unity.

"In the world you will have tribulation, but be of good cheer, I have conquered the world" (16:33). The past tense is appropriate, because Jesus has already won the spiritual victory in principle (12:27-36). It also expresses certitude with regard to the future, when the redemptive work of Christ will be that accomplished which continually gives assurance to the Church. At the very moment when Christ is face to face with treachery and disgrace and death, he triumphantly claims victory. In his victory his followers conquer also. The end of Christ's words is that we may have peace, not ease, but victory.

Jesus is very concerned to prevent their distress when they see the tragic events a few hours hence. Also the whole Paschal discourse and especially the present Ch 16 has specifically been designed to calm these timorous disciples in face of provocation. The world, as the great outer ring of human experience, will move this way and that; but at the center, in Christ, is the stable compass directing their way into the peace of God. And because the will of the world has already exposed itself, Jesus could consider it defeated in principle already. There only remains his love which he pours out in prayer (Ch 17) for his friends and the world he came to redeem.

9

CHRIST'S PRIESTLY PRAYER I

Christ prays for himself (17:1-5), for his disciples (6-19), and for those who will believe through the disciples mission (20-26).

The time for sacrifice draws near. In his priestly prayer (Ch 17) Jesus offers himself and intercedes for his disciples. The three characteristics of the gospel, simplicity, subtlety, and sublimity reach a climax here. This chapter is perhaps the simplest in language yet the profoundest in meaning, in the whole Bible. It contains what has been called the high-priestly prayer of Jesus, sometimes the prayer of consecration, sometimes the intercessory prayer. It is difficult to find a phrase that suitably describes it. That it is a prayer is clear from the opening verses, yet it is a prayer to which we have no precise parallel in the gospels. It is more an outpouring of the soul of Jesus as in the presence of his Father, than a series of petitions addressed, like so many of our prayers, to a Being dwelling in remote and transcendent splendor. Here Christ's words are addressed directly to the Father rather than to the disciples, who only overhear. Although still in the world (13), Jesus looks on his earthly ministry as a thing of the past (4, 12). And whereas he has hitherto stated that the disciples could not follow him (13:33, 36), now he wishes them to be with him in union with the Father (12-13). He is crossing the threshold of eternity.

The title high-priestly prayer is apt, for this is Christ's prayer consecrating his body and blood for the sacrifice in which they are about to be offered, and his benediction over the Church that he is to bring forth in his glorification. Although the synoptics frequently picture Jesus in prayer, especially on occasions of greater importance such as this, only rarely is the content of his prayer given. As we might expect, this prayer sums up the signification of Christ's life. It is his consecration of himself as the mediator of salvation. It expresses exactly what the author of Hebrews projected of his eternal intercession: "He is able for all time to save those who draw near to God through him, since he always lives to make intercession for them" (Heb 7:25).

As the high priest on the Day of Atonement, the great annual feast of the Jews (Lv 16), prayed for himself, for the priests and the Levites, and for the whole congregation of Israel, so now Jesus prays for himself, for the disciples, and for all future believers. It is a record of Jesus' self-consecration as it lived in the memory of his intimate disciple, and it falls into three parts: the Son and the Father (1-8); the Son and the disciples (9-19); the Son, the disciples and the world (20-26).

It is unlike the high priest's prayer on the Atonement Day in that there is no mention of sin or pleading for forgiveness. It is the prayer of the faithful high priest of the good things that are to come (Heb 2:17); it is the offering of human life at its best; of his own accomplished work, of the Apostles' acceptance of him and allegiance, of the faith of their converts and of the whole world. It is a prayer for support and further protection and sanctification. The Son thanks the Father for all his gifts and for the work which he has enabled him to do in expressing the Father's love in human life; but he prays for further help; death lies before him, may he be strengthened to glorify the Father, to show his love for man in that; may he be carried through it to that union with the Father which will enable him in yet fuller measure to unite men to himself and through him to the Father, in a life of love and truth, until the whole world comes to believe.

The priestly prayer deserves its name. Jesus mentions his consecration (17:19) only once but the whole prayer is bathed in an atmosphere of sacrifice. According to his promise (14:16) he inaugurates his office of intercession which he will continue in heaven. On this last night he realizes in his person under the eyes of his apostles the different aspects of the priesthood. *Absolute devotedness to the service of the brethren:* the Master washes their feet. *The ministry of the word:* the Incarnate Word exhorts his disciples as today in the Christian assembly, the priest proclaims the gospel message. *Prayer:* it is not sufficient to instruct people, the priest must also obtain by prayer, the grace to understand Christian teaching and put it into practice. Moreover, Jesus prays in a special way for priests (17:9) expressing his most intimate feelings and indicating what esteem we should have for the priesthood. Finally, Jesus proposes to us a type of liturgical supplication, which can be compared to the Canon of the Mass. It was the solemn prayer which accompanied the sacrifice of the cross. Briefly, our Lord offers us not only a rule of action (Ch 13-16) but also a rule of prayer (Ch 17), a complete rule of life. The priestly existence demands both action and prayer. The apostle is a contemplative in action, one whose very action is contemplative.

The ideal priestly prayer is that of God's Son, ever dwelling on the righteous, holy character of his Father (1, 11, 24, 25), recognizing that all that he has is a gift from the Father and must be given by him to others (note that the word, to give, occurs seventeen times). The prayers are for others in order of responsibility for them (himself, those nearest to him, all believers, the world); praying for their protection and growth, and realizing that such growth can only reach perfection in union with each other and with God.

This prayer is suitably called Christ's priestly prayer, because in it he solemnly consecrates himself to be priest and victim in the approaching sacrifice. The veil is drawn back for the moment from the inner sanctuary of his mind, and we are enabled to contemplate with awe and reverence the nature of that close communion which he had habitually with the heavenly Father. This is the priest-victim's oblation-intercession, on the eve of his sacrifice, asking that his work may continue through those whom the Father had given him, in a unity of charity that shares in the unity of the Father and the Son (20-23), a unity holy, apostolic, universal (19-20) to be consummated in eternal love. This preface to the historical sacrifice of the cross is chanted by the Son as he is about to pass the threshold of eternity, and enter into his glory in the bosom of the Father. He speaks at times as if still in the world (17:13, 19), at times as if his ministry were past (11-12, 18). The sweating victim falling face to earth in the prayer of the agony (Mk 14:35) is in striking contrast to the Son lifting up his eyes to heaven. But the same priest-victim speaks in both (Jn 17:19).

Consecration is the key thought which pervades the whole Ch 17. Jesus presents himself as consecrated for his great sacrifice of love and obedience; as both victim and priest of this sacrifice, he prays for all the fruits that will derive from it. First Jesus prays for himself that the crowning act of his earthly ministry may indeed lead to the glorious conclusion which God has intended (17:1-5). Next he prays for his disciples, that they may be protected and upheld in their mission, which is the continuation of his own (6-19). It is in connection with the mission that Jesus uses the language of sacrifice which has earned the whole piece the title of consecration prayer. After this it is entirely natural that Jesus should go on to pray for the Church of the future, which will be the fruit of the disciples' mission (20-23). Here the whole emphasis falls on the overriding need to maintain the unity of the Christian community, echoing the new commandment of 13:34-35. Finally, Jesus prays for the union of all, both the disciples and the Church of the future, in his ultimate glory in the presence of the Father, thus drawing together the threads of all three preceding sections (24-26).

Jesus' high priestly prayer falls naturally into three parts. Jesus prays for himself (17:1-5). The hour of Jesus' perfect obedience unto death has come, securing eternal life for men through knowledge (personal acquaintance) of God and his

Son. Having accomplished his work, Jesus awaits the restoration of his pre-incarnate glory. Jesus' prayer for his disciples (6-19) left in the world after his ascension, is that they may be one as are the Father and the Son (11), have joy (13), be victorious over the evil one (15) and fulfill the mission of representing Christ to the world (16-19). Jesus' prayer for the Church (20-26) is that it may be indwelt by the Father and the Son and express their unity in love, thus fulfilling its mission of leading the world to believe.

Christ prays for himself, that as he has glorified the Father by his life on earth, so he may also glorify him by his death, and after death may receive again that glory which for our sake he resigned at his incarnation. For the apostles, that they may be kept from sin, and from unfaithfulness in the midst of a wicked and hostile world, that they may be united in affection and will, and that they may be consecrated, even as he is consecrated, for the solemn mission which they are to undertake. For the world, that it may be converted; for believers that they may have perfect union and communion, visible and invisible, with one another, in virtue of their union with the one God through the one Christ; and that, finally, all may attain to everlasting salvation and see Christ enthroned in that glory he had with the Father before the world was. The prayer has four focuses of concern: Jesus' offering of himself for his Father's purposes (17:1-5); his concern for the destiny of his disciples after his ascension (6-19); the outreach of intercession to all future believers until the end of time (20-23); and the expectation of the final consummation in the age to come (24-26).

This is no short-hand report, but a synthesis which may have had in view the Eucharistic celebration of John's day. Yet a prayer accompanied the Last Supper and the fundamental elements of this prayer go back to this historic event: namely, the reference to the hour, the contacts with the Bread of Life discourse, Jesus' care for his own who are to remain in the world, his allusion to the treason, the mission of the disciples, and his self-consecration to death. Taking its origin from the act of salvation (17:1-5)—the prayer passes through the medium of the apostles (6-19) to all generations (20-23) and the end of time (24). In the flight of the Spirit, John's gaze embraces the eternity of the beginning and the eternity of the consummation. In substance the prayer is a true transcript of the mind of Jesus when confronted with his approaching death on the cross. The certitude of the Father's presence and of the Father's will which throbs through the whole prayer is the certitude of Jesus himself. The consciousness of his own mission revealed in this prayer is that which pervades the whole gospel. The sense of the task awaiting his disciples in the world is wholly akin to the mind of Jesus as already manifested. All this, we cannot but feel, is a transcript from the consciousness of the historic Jesus. From what we know of the inmost mind of Jesus, we may say that this is the kind of prayer we should expect him to make.

Communion with God reaches visible expression in the practice of prayer. This is no less true of the Son of God, whose unity with the Father is, in his incarnate life expressed in prayer, and supremely as far as the fourth gospel is concerned in this prayer. It is for this reason that the prayer sums up what has been delivered about the work of Christ in other forms in other parts of the gospel. It emphasizes his obedience to the Father; the fact that his obedient death reveals the glory of God; the choice of the disciples out of the world; the revelation made to them; their unity in love; and their eternal dwelling in Christ and in God. The prayer focuses and recapitulates the central thoughts of the Gospel.

The few prayers of Jesus recorded in the synoptics are invariably short and addressed with intimate immediacy to his Father. The two examples hitherto in this gospel (11:41-42 and 12:27) share these characteristics, and each of them is a cry of Jesus at a moment of great tension. The extended prayer of this chapter is more serene and meditative, gathering up the themes of the preceding discourse. It is both a final resolution of Jesus' obedience to the death which will be his glorification, and an intercession for the fruits of his accomplished work after his ascension. Much of what is usually called the Lord's Prayer is heard in this chapter, notably the sense of the divine Father, whose name is to be hallowed, whose will is to be done, whose children are to be guarded in the hour of temptation and kept from evil. That these were the burden of our Lord's thought in his intercessory fellowship with the Father is clear. And that they are the leading themes of this prayer is also clear to anyone who will meditate on it.

The prayer is thus primarily an act of intercession. It fittingly concludes the account of the Last Supper, summing up as it does the whole purpose of John's presentation of the narrative, in which the meaning of discipleship has been the dominant theme. As for its literary type, the prayer is a final, farewell message, a sort of last will and testament. This literary device of a final message is found in the Bible itself: Jacob, Moses, Deuteronomy, Samuel, Paul. It is a device whereby the author hopes to produce moral effect by the emotional impact of the situation. Here Jesus is inculcating his unique position in relation to men, so that they may live in union with him. And this is a moral union carrying with it mutual obligations. It is a unity which is modelled on the relation of Jesus to the Father himself.

It could well be that the evangelist thinks of this prayer as the model of the Church's *Eucharistic* intercession. For the prayer was uttered on the night of the institution of the Eucharist; it expresses the spirit of the Eucharist, the Church's divinely ordered ceremonial method of self-identification with the sacrifice of Christ. There the Church offers its praise and thanksgiving for all God's gifts to it throughout the past, especially the human life and death of the Son; there it thinks of him as offering himself for the salvation of the whole world; it pleads the entire self-sacrifice as its ideal; it prays to be united with it and to be able to go forth to a life of faith in the truth, and of the services of love, sharing the joy of its Lord, until the whole world shall believe.

10

CHRIST'S PRIESTLY PRAYER II

From Ch 13 to 16 Jesus has unfolded the meaning of his departure. His teaching ends with the words, "I have overcome the world," meaning that ultimately it could be said that, in him, the purpose of God had been, and will be achieved. So with his eyes lifted towards heaven, Jesus terminates his work on earth, and contemplates his work as a priest, entering in spirit, the Holy Place. The action of looking up to heaven and the address *Father* are typical of Jesus at prayer. The gesture is repeated in many liturgies. Though John for his own reasons has omitted any direct reference to the Eucharist in his account of the Last Supper, a prayer such as Ch 17 would have accompanied it most appropriately.

The final part of the Last Supper discourse of Jesus takes the form of a prayer, but in it his instruction certainly continues. The prayer is for the consummation of all that he has been speaking of to the disciples, of the union between them and himself, the union which consists in faith and in love of the disciple for him and the Father. So first of all he prays for himself, and for himself in union with the Father, the union which signifies and makes possible the unity of the Church with Christ (17:1-5).

The prayer begins with our Lord's customary address to God, "Father." All the teaching of Jesus was controlled by the sense of the Father's presence, and the mission given him to fulfill. That mission was now on the verge of consummation. The hour was come. The sense of impending consummation has dominated the mind of Jesus throughout these last chapters. It is an hour of glorification. So intimate and sure is the certitude of the Father's presence possessed by Jesus, that in spite of the evil agency of men, he regards that glorification of himself in sacrificial death as the fulfillment of the Father's own purpose, and the means of the Father's own glorification. When the Father glorifies the Son, the Son glorifies the Father. When the Son offers himself, the Father is seen for what he essentially is. The cross, in revealing a perfect filial relationship, reveals also the Father's own nature. This is a prayer of acknowledgement and of acceptance. Jesus acknowledges the divine will for him and accepts it. This is the essence of all true prayer. To God alone the glory, Thy will, not mine, be done.

Jesus prays for his own glorification. Jewish hope was directed to the hour of God's definitive intervention at the end of time; determined by the Father, Jesus' hour is constantly on the horizon of his activity, and he recognizes it and accepts it deliberately. It is the moment of the glorification of the Son of Man. But this glorification is effected by perfect obedience, by love, in the humiliation of the cross; this is the way Christ glorifies the Father.

Jesus' intercession has a high-priestly character reminiscent of Rm 8:34 and Heb. He does not really pray for himself, except perhaps in v. 5, but for the completion of his mission, to reveal the unseen God, who can be seen in the Son. Divine acceptance of his sacrifice will redeem men to the glory of the Father, whose glory is one with his. Jesus prays that his approaching death may prove to be the means by which the Father and Son are mutually glorified in the completion of the work of redemption. It is by the Passion that the Son will exercise the authority he possesses over all mankind, and the purpose of his authority is the giving of eternal life which the Father has committed to him.

Christ asks the Father to glorify him by accepting the sacrifice of his death and by raising him from the dead. When this is done, the Son will glorify the Father by converting the world. He has glorified the Father by the words and deeds of his earthly life, and now he will continue to glorify him in the extension of his person, in the Church, in the lives of those whom he will bring to sanctity. In his glorification Jesus will glorify the Father by the gift of eternal life, for this will beget for God new children who honor him as Father (1:12). Thus in his request to return to his heavenly home, Jesus really does not seek anything for himself; he is interested in the recognition of his Father and the welfare of his disciples.

"Father, the hour has come, glorify your Son that the Son may glorify you. You gave him power to give eternal life to all whom you gave him" (17:2). The particular act of power that will make visible the unity of Jesus and the Father will be the gift of eternal life to believers. The glorification of Christ implies the power to associate to his new condition all who are under the influence of the Father and are prepared to receive the divine word. At the Incarnation the Father gave the Son authority to die for the sins of the whole world, and to proclaim the Father's gracious offer of salvation to all mankind. Those whom the Father gives to Christ are those who freely accept the offer of salvation which is freely made to all. Eternal life is John's regular substitute for the kingdom of God of earlier tradition. It is therefore true that the first verses of the prayer correspond with the opening of the Lord's prayer: "Our Father, who art in heaven, hallowed be thy name. Thy kingdom come." Here the prayer is more urgent and insistent. The success of God's plan for all mankind hangs upon this moment. This consideration thus anticipates the prayer for the disciples and the Church which is to follow.

"This is eternal life, that they know you the only true God, and Jesus Christ whom you have sent" (17:3). Eternal life is the main theme of John's gospel. It is here defined as arising out of and consisting in the knowledge of God. But for John the knowledge of the only true God is incomplete without reference to "Jesus Christ whom you have sent;" that is, it is only possible to speak satisfactorily of the knowledge of God in the context of the historic mission of Jesus. Eternal life consists in the immediate knowledge (which implies mutual knowledge) of the Father, which can be obtained only through the knowledge of Christ in whom is revealed the supreme manifestation of the unique God.

The joy of the early Church shines out in John's description of eternal life. To know implies intimate, loving union, continuously growing. It is equally eternal life to know the glorious Son whom the Father sent to reveal him. "Gloria Dei vivens homo; vita autem hominis visio Dei" (St. Irenaeus Haer 4, 20). In biblical language, knowledge is not merely the conclusion of an intellectual process but the fruit of a personal experience, a personal contact; when it matures it is love. Knowledge of God is not mere theological erudition. It is especially personal communion, an I-Thou encounter with God such as is described for example in Ps 139. Nor is John speaking of a double knowledge, as though one began with the knowledge of the true God and then went on to gain knowledge of Christ. It is one knowledge of God, one fellowship with him, that comes through Christ.

The human nature of Jesus never rose to a higher point than in this prayer. The purpose of his supreme dedication of himself is that his disciples should have eternal life. Eternal life is defined as knowing God as he is revealed in his Son; to know him as their Father, as Jesus knew him as his Father. Hitherto the Mosaic law had been the instrument of revelation which now comes to man through Christ. The knowledge of the Father must be linked now with the apprehension of the Son, since the revelation of God in Christ cannot be transcended. This again is not mere intellectual understanding, but the perfection of personal, moral trust.

Jesus now gives the grounds for his urgent demand (17:4-5). There are two stages in his mission of revealing God. First there is the whole of his work on earth. This has been accomplished. Now it must be followed by the second stage, the glorification of the Son of Man, without which it remains incomplete and unconvincing. Jesus has achieved his life's aim of glorifying the Father by completing the work of our redemption which he was sent to do. He asks that his suffering humanity may achieve, in the Father's bosom, the glory which the Father eternally decreed in the incarnation

(1:14) and which belongs to his eternal existence as Son (8:58). Christ's glory was manifested throughout his early life, but appears in all its splendor starting with his resurrection and makes him henceforth the one par excellence who manifests the Father's name. This is no selfish request for recognition. Rather it is a prayer which already recognizes that the historic life-giving work of Christ may truly reveal the eternal nature of the Godhead, and the relation of the Word, immanent and active in creation and salvation, to the eternal and unchanging transcendent God. The passage gives expression to that unique sense of the presence of the Father possessed by Jesus, by which he transcended the categories of time and space. His consciousness (we speak with reverent diffidence) should not be regarded as a memory of a pre-temporal existence; it was rather a present assurance of the eternal Father. The language of time expresses a consciousness of eternity. The idea of a qualitative completeness of life is conveyed by the idea of priority. The glory of the Son of Man is a matter of intimate personal relationship, rather than splendid robes and royal state. In the final reckoning, it can be expressed in terms of love.

Jesus renders God an account of his stewardship (17:6-8). To the men God gave him he has made known God's name, that is, revealed his fatherly nature and purpose; and they have responded with obedience, so that they now know with certainty that their master is from God. To them he has revealed the name, that is, the nature and character of God. What they have learned is that the mission of Jesus is from God; that is, that God is to be known in Jesus Christ, and that the work of Jesus is to be understood as the work of God. Though often lacking in understanding, the disciples have been faithful to the teaching given them, even as Jesus was faithful to his commission from the Father (8:55). The evidence for this took two forms: knowledge and faith, in both cases centered on the divine origin of the mission of Jesus. The disciples have accepted the full implications of the revelation of God in Jesus. It is thus put most emphatically that they recognize the source of Jesus' sayings in God himself. "Know in truth" and "have believed" are not to be distinguished as if knowledge was different from blind faith. Both verbs express appropriation of divine truth with the heart and mind and will. So also "I came from you" and "you sent me" are completely synonymous ways of expressing the incarnation.

11

CHRIST'S PRIESTLY PRAYER III

Jesus' prayer for his disciples (17:9-19) has four petitions. First Jesus prays the Holy Father to protect the disciples by his gracious providence, by the power of his name, so "that they may be one, as we are one" (11). One, like Father and Son, in heart and purpose; for lacking this unity, their mission must fail. Second (13) he prays that they may know fully the joy of accomplished work, which has been his. This will compensate for the world's hatred which will surely be theirs for their loyalty to Christ. Third (15) he prays that even while exposed to the perils of living in the world, they may be kept from evil. Lastly (17) he prays God to "consecrate them by the truth." Consecration here means being equipped, or made fit, for divine service. This will be theirs as they are brought into the truth which is the word, or revelation of God. So they will be fitted for the work to which he is now sending them.

Christ's prayer on behalf of his disciples is an extension of the prayer for his own glorification (1); for it is in the perseverance and mission of these disciples that the name of God will be glorified. Just as God has revealed his glory in Jesus (13:31), so the disciples will reveal the glory of Jesus. On behalf of his disciples Jesus urges three motives: they now belong more intimately to the Father, since they are the Son's very own, and Son and Father have all in common; he has been and is glorified by them and they will spread his glory; and finally, they will be left alone in the world. It is for his disciples that Jesus prays, not for the world. This does not mean that the world is past praying for, as the saying goes. Are we not told that "God loved the world so much that he gave his only Son" to save it? It means that the world's only hope is that it should cease being what it is, and become like the disciples, the property of God and his Christ (Rv 11:15).

"Holy Father, keep them in your name, those you have given me, that they may be one, even as we are one" (17:11). Keep them in your name as a place of security, that is, keep them safe as being your own; in your name, by the power of your divine name giving protection. This name is incarnate in the Son; the divine nature possessed in common by Father and Son is the source and model of the disciples' unity with God and with one another. They must be kept in God's name, with the word and life which Jesus has bestowed on them. They must "be one even as we are one," preserved in a love that has as its measure the love of the Father for the Son.

The holiness of the Father is the foundation of the holiness of Jesus and of the disciples which will be mentioned later (17, 19). The invocation "Holy Father" was utilized very early in the Christian liturgy. The adjective *holy* appears in view of the theme of holiness in the substance of the prayer (14-19). Holy expresses separation from the profane, and in God the highest perfection of purity. "Holy Father" introduces the prayer for the disciples to be preserved from contagion (11, 15) and consecrated, like Jesus, to God's service and love (17). Holy is the antithesis of all that the world stands for.

As Israel was a holy nation because God chose it to convey to the world the knowledge of himself, so the Holy Father is entreated to keep those whom Jesus has guarded for this end, that they may be sanctified, separate, made God's own, "in the truth," which is equivalent to "in the name" (11) with emphasis on the idea that God is the only true God. The adjective holy is suitable, though in fact rare in invocation of God. Here it is perhaps an anticipation of the theme of consecration with which the prayer for the disciples will conclude (17-19), just as "righteous" (25) is related to the content of the prayer.

May the Father of all holiness, that is the burden of the prayer, keep in his own sanctity these disciples; that their unity in mind and endeavor may be the spiritual unity already existing between himself and the Father. Their oneness is no spurious, or spectacular union, such as men delude themselves in thinking they have, when they obliterate diversities in the interests of mechanical uniformity. It is unity of mind and purpose. The real difficulty from which Jesus wished his disciples to be delivered was undesirable diversity caused by the sectarian spirit, not the desirable diversity caused by the manifoldness of the gifts of God to his children.

Unity in mutual love is the consequence of the union which unites the Father and the Son (21-23). The unity of the Father and the Son (10:30) is the model and principle of the unity of the disciples, since the name that Christ has revealed is nothing less than the divine life itself. By receiving him who reveals the name of the Father, the disciples have themselves entered into such a communion with him that no earthly power will henceforth be able to separate them from him.

Up to now Jesus himself strove to keep his little ones around him and guarded them as their shepherd. He now prays that the eleven who are left may come to a full knowledge of his own joy. Such a joy consists in having the word of Jesus, that is, in having his essential mind and spirit. No one can know the joy of service but one who serves, nor the joy of humility but one who is humble, nor the joy of sacrifice but one who offers himself. Joy is a product of the spirit. Jesus prays that his disciples may share to the full his joy as he returns to the bosom of the Father. No more exalted prospect could be conceived. The joy of hearing the word of Jesus (3:29) reaches its fullness when no work of the world can really menace our union with the Father.

"I do not pray that you should take them out of the world, but that you should keep them from evil" (17:15). Reacting against a passive expectation of the Parousia, this saying underlines that the task of the Christian community is to be among men the manifestation of the eschatological world. This task supposes necessarily the confrontation with the

powers of evil and of hatred, which can be conquered only
with the help of the Father. Jesus is not wanting an escape-
route for his disciples but preservation in an adverse
environment. Those with a mission to the world must be in it
as leaven and not in ivory towers; but Jesus knows the danger
they run and prays that they be not infected. Our Lord's ideal
is not freedom from work, but strength to do it; not freedom
from suffering but joy in an abiding sense of the Father's love;
not absence from the world, but grace to make it better by our
presence; not holy lives driven from the world, and living apart
from it, but holy lives spent in the world and leavening it.

In Jn 17:17-19 Jesus speaks of his dedication, his
consecration to his mission, which is the ground of the
dedication of the disciples to theirs. Consecration means
being equipped, or made fit, for a divine service. This will be
theirs as they are brought into the truth, which is the word or
revelation of God. But as verse 19 shows, consecration
involves more than this. Consecrate, a sacrificial term, means
to set apart for a holy purpose what is flawless. And when
Jesus says "for their sake I consecrate myself," he is referring
to the offering of his own sinless life to God on the cross. This
offering he says is "for their sake, that they too may be
consecrated in truth," that is that they may serve God as truly
dedicated men.

Jesus asks God to consecrate them to their apostolic
office, endowing them with divine illumination and wisdom
for their work. Our Lord was consecrated for his work when
he entered the world (10:36) so now he consecrates his
disciples before he sends them forth (17:18). Now once more
he consecrates himself, not this time as a mere teacher, but
as priest and victim in the approaching sacrifice. The blood of
the covenant, which his death will initiate and ratify, will
consecrate his apostles to their office and work. The disciples
are the priests of the new law. Just as the priests of the old
law were consecrated, made holy, so are those of the new, but
in a more personal and intimate way. The word of God himself
(14) which is truth is their consecration. And Christ surely

means that this work of consecration will be done by the Spirit of truth (16:13).

"Sanctify them in the truth; your word is the truth" (17:17). Consecration or sanctification is the separation of a being from the domain of the profane and the complete introduction into the godly sphere. Sanctification is thus also the work of the Holy Father. The word consecrate expresses God's destination of them for their work and his endowment of them with the power necessary for it. The word is used of God's consecration of Jeremiah, Moses, and the chosen people. This prayer (17:17) is aptly called the prayer of consecration.

Not only is the relation of Father and Son the model of the disciple-and-Christ relationship, it is its principle. They must be consecrated with a priestly consecration, not, however, with anything less than the consecration of the Son himself, of truth and the word. The instrument of sanctification is God's truth manifested in the Incarnate Word to whom the disciples adhere by faith; it is God's revelation of his word, penetrating and transforming them. To be consecrated in the truth is then to live in the realm of the spirit where Jesus has his home. There is only truth where there is sanctity, and only sanctity where there is truth.

"As you sent me into the world, so I have sent them into the world" (17:18). To fulfill so high a calling will require the utmost loyalty and devotion. So now Jesus prays that they may not fail to profit by his own example of self-sacrifice. Their consecration-sanctification renders the disciples capable of fulfilling their mission because it set them apart from the world without isolating them, making them bearers of the Christ's words with the help of the Holy Spirit in their witnessing. The mission of Christ and the apostolic mission of the Church are one and the same, drawing their resources from the same source, with the same authority and power. It is to the end that they should truly be consecrated in the whole service that lies before them that Christ devotes himself in sacrificial death.

"And for their sake I consecrate myself that they also may be sanctified in truth" (17:19). "I consecrate myself" expresses Jesus' self-offering to God through his death. He offers his sacrifice for his followers. He sanctifies himself by presenting himself before the Father to be one with him, and before men as God's perfect revelation. He prays that his disciples live in God's truth, sanctified by the faith in the Father which has been revealed to them. Their sanctification is based ultimately on the sacrifice of the cross and on the gift of the Spirit by the risen Christ. The strictly sacrificial aspect is accentuated by the formula "for their sake" and by the proximity of the passion. Jesus expresses his will of freely offering his life for the consecration of his disciples. This verse is a highlight in Christ's priestly prayer. Christ does for himself that which he prays the Father to do for his disciples. In 10:36 he speaks of himself as consecrated by the Father, set apart for a sacred purpose. As a priest consecrated by the Father, Christ consecrates himself as sacrifice (Ep 5:2), and thereby obtains a real internal consecration for them through the Paraclete (16:7). He is to become a high priest forever in virtue of his sacrificial death. And the truth is related to Christ's death, so far as the disciples are concerned, in that their ministry will only be relevant if it is colored by the implications of his death.

The prepositional phrase "for their sake" unmistakably introduces a sacrificial connotation. John has used it in the context of laying down one's life in the shepherd allegory (10:11), in the unwitting prophecy of Caiphas (11:51), and in the vine allegory (15:13). He has also used it in an allusion to the Eucharistic words of Jesus (6:51). It is quite possible that its presence here is a reminiscence of the Eucharist. Jesus offers himself as a sacrifice on their behalf. This again suggests that John is building on the tradition of the Eucharistic words which he paraphrases for the present context.

Finally Jesus prays (17:20-26) for those who will believe his disciples' word, in particular that they all may be one (20-23). The future body of believers is regarded as already in existence; the apostles are a guarantee and an earnest of the Church that is to be. "That they all may be one as you Father are in me and I in you, that they also may be one in us so that the world may believe that you sent me" (17:21). Christian unity finds its ideal in the unity between the Father and the Son, in a personal relationship of mutual love, not in some mere external incorporation. Believers are thus so united among themselves that they become for the world the sign par excellence of God's eschatological intervention of the authenticity of Jesus' mission. Christian unity and love is a moral miracle, a conquest of the resisting will of man, and therefore more convincing than a physical miracle, which is a conquest of unresisting nature. Hence the divisions and animosities of Christians are a perpetual stumbling-block to the world. The only deadly schism in the New Testament is to be separated in spirit and in aim from the living Christ. The disciples form a circle of love which includes both the Father and the Son. The existence of any part of the circle witnesses to the whole. The center of Christian unity is not on earth but in heaven. Christians are one, because they are spiritually united to the Father and the Son, whose divine life and blessed union they share by faith that gives eternal life, and through believing participation in the sacraments.

The final prayer (17:24-26) summarizes the purpose of Christ's coming into the world and of his setting apart of his disciples. The vista is that of eternity. Finally, believers are not to be left in the world (11); they are to be with Christ, sharing the eternal love and glory of the Godhead. This is a prayer that the Church militant may become the Church triumphant.

"I have made known your name to them, and I will make it known that the love with which you loved me may be in them, and I in them" (17:26). The whole purpose of revelation is that the Father's love for Christ, the Son may indwell the disciples. Love is Jesus' supreme goal and final desire. By his use of inclusion (13:1) the beloved disciple has chosen to set all these chapters under the leitmotif of love. "I in them" is the last aspiration of Jesus for his own before he sets forth to meet death. In these words alone, everything is said. The prayer ends with the assurance of the indwelling of Christ in believers. It ends with the substance of the new commandment now raised to the status of the theological justification of the entire work of redemption. These last words sum up the purpose of Christ's prayer. They are the thread that runs through the entire discourse. He is going away and yet abides with them. His earthly presence passes away, his spiritual presence remains forever, not seen with the eye without, but felt as light and strength within.